Tough Gynes

TOUGH GYNES

Violent Women in Film as Honorary Men

Stan Goff

CASCADE *Books* • Eugene, Oregon

TOUGH GYNES
Violent Women in Film as Honorary Men

Cascade Books
An Imprint of Wipf and Stock Publishers
199 W. 8th Ave., Suite 3
Eugene, OR 97401

www.wipfandstock.com

PAPERBACK ISBN: 978-1-5326-4408-5
HARDCOVER ISBN: 978-1-5326-4409-2
EBOOK ISBN: 978-1-5326-4410-8

Cataloguing-in-Publication data:

Names: Goff, Stan.

Title: Tough gynes : violent women in film as honorary men / Stan Goff.

Description: Eugene, OR : Cascade Books, 2019 | Includes bibliographical references and index.

Identifiers: ISBN 978-1-5326-4408-5 (paperback) | ISBN 978-1-5326-4409-2 (hardcover) | ISBN 978-1-5326-4410-8 (ebook)

Subjects: LCSH: Violence in mass media. | Feminism. | Violence—Sex differences. | Sex role in mass media. | Mass media and culture. | Christian Ethics.

Classification: P96.V5 G64 2019 (print) | P96.V5 G64 (ebook)

Manufactured in the U.S.A. 03/05/19

The Light shines in the darkness, and the darkness does not comprehend it.

—John 1:5

Elatus's daughter, Caenis, loveliest of the virgins of Thessaly, was famous for her beauty, a girl longed for in vain, the object of many suitors throughout the neighboring cities and your own (since she was one of your people, Achilles). Perhaps Peleus also would have tried to wed her, but he had already taken your mother in marriage, or she was promised to your father. Caenis would not agree to any marriage, but (so rumor has it) she was walking along a lonely beach, and the god took her by force. When Neptune had enjoyed his new love he said: "Make your wish, without fear of refusal. Ask for what you most want!"

"This injury evokes the great desire never to be able to suffer any such again. Grant I might not be a woman: you will have given me everything," Caenis said. She spoke the last words in a deeper tone, that might have been the sound of a man's voice. So it was: the god of the deep ocean had already accepted her wish, and had granted, over and above it, that as a man Caeneus would be protected from all wounds, and never fall to the sword. Caeneus, the Atracides, left, happy with his gifts, and spent his time in manly pastimes, roaming the Thessalian fields.

—Ovid's *Metamorphoses*, Book VII

A commitment to sexual equality with men is a commitment to becoming the rich instead of the poor, the rapist instead of the raped, the murderer instead of the murdered.

—Andrea Dworkin

Contents

Preface

Borderline was published in February 2015, a book in which I argued that war and masculinity are part of a self-reproducing reciprocal feedback loop. War produces violent masculinity, which in turn reproduces war. Cascade Books graciously published it, and the sheer size of the thing raised the cost of the book above fifty dollars. I had also overwhelmed all but the most intrepid of readers with the interdisciplinary scope of it—history, theology, psychoanalysis, virtue ethics, gender theory, literary criticism, autobiographical anecdotes . . . *Borderline* has it all. I'm still happy with the book, and I'm not saying people ought not to read it. By all means, buy copies for everyone in your family as gifts. My little truck is twenty-seven years old and drives like a sloppy tractor. If friends and family won't read it, it's still big enough to make an attractive and interesting doorstop.

In February 2017, two years later, as I was working on *Mammon's Ecology*, also for Cascade, my editor Charlie Collier emailed me with the suggestion that we take some of the sub-themes of *Borderline* and turn them into smaller, more accessible books, to reach beyond *Borderline*'s readers. This book is the first fruit of that very sound suggestion.

One of the most common arguments in response to *Borderline*, and consistently in discussions I've observed over two decades now of immersion in controversies surrounding sex as practice and gender as power structure,[1] is that my claims and the claims of several feminists are becoming outdated because women have made tremendous advancements over the years, especially with regard to filling roles that were formerly and nearly exclusively

1. We're going to employ a clumsy, hyphenated phrase from here forward: sex-gender. It's not pretty, but it is a reminder that the sex and gender distinction often underwrites a larger nature-culture distinction that exists only in our minds and never in reality.

filled by men. Not so fast, I say. Because the subtext here often seems to be, let's apply the brakes before this equality stuff goes too far.

When I use the term "gender" in this book, I am referring to a set of *social structures* that divide power unequally between men and women. There is another use for the word "gender," which is a category that includes all the various forms of sexual difference, personal and cultural—a vaguely post-Nietzschean notion that incorporates "identity," "representation," and "performance."[2] So for *this* book, remember: gender means the *difference in power*, and it is expressed through the cultural association of men with "masculinity" and women with "femininity." This book is, however, about several performances, in the actual theatric sense.

Sex-gender is complicated in the same way that discussions of race are complicated inasmuch as there is truth in this assertion that some forms of injustice have been overcome. Sexual harassment is now a crime, and interracial couples show up on television ads without white riots. But these facts can serve to mask the myriad ways in which gender and race—as unjust social structures that separate power—continue to operate beyond these obvious improvements. "It can look like a duck," as my old pal Daisy Duckhunter used to say, "but it could be a decoy."

The social movements that broke legal segregation in the United States were a Good Thing, as is the fact that law schools and medical schools now enroll many women. Rape, in its strictest definition, is now prosecutable *within* marriage, which once was not the case. People of

2. People's actions interpreted as "performance" is an easy idea to share in our own epoch, and it is shared widely and uncritically even within the Academy. *Performance* calls to mind actions taken before an audience, self-consciously fabricating our every posture, gesture, and word to convey something to observers. We all know, for example, how the introduction of a camera alters our behavior, how it makes us self-conscious, taking our minds off the objectives of our actions and fixing our consciousness instead on how we appear. When film and, especially, television came on the scene, we began to see actors and other public figures—who were always performing when we saw them—as (and here is a telling theater term) "role" models. I argue that prior to the introduction of the ever more ubiquitous camera, this was not part of a dominant episteme except for politicians and the like, public figures, con artists, and so on, whose job was to manipulate the public. The only reason we can get away with notions like "gender performance" is because we have naturalized this lack of sincerity, this self-conscious acting, which is profoundly alienating, as a way of living, as our primary waking experience. Performance has been further naturalized by psychologists influenced by Nietzsche (like Erving Goffman) who essentially deny that an authentic "self" exists, rewriting human beings as "subjectivities" without any actual subjects. That naturalization needs to be called into question, especially in a book about film performances and how they affect social life.

any ethnicity can now intermarry without crosses being burned on their lawns. Lots of young people I know hang out effortlessly with "different" folks, when, during my own youth, we had to stretch pretty hard across those boundaries to establish friendships. Good stuff. Real stuff. Worthy of our affirmation . . . and vigilance.

At the same time, an African American President did not substantially improve the lot of *most* African Americans, a few female CEOs have not substantially improved the lot of *most* women, and the violent power structures that preceded the incorporation—literally—of female persons and persons of color into those same power structures has not changed the fundamentally violent and unjust character of these structures. In fact, these symbolic victories can actually stunt our ability to effectively recognize and criticize the violence, injustice, and historic "masculinity" of those structures.

"It can look like a duck, but it could be a decoy."

A transnational corporation can pollute air, land, and water, acquire raw materials from the hellish landscapes of East Asian sweatshops or African mines, and still be publicly congratulated for its first black/woman/Latin@ CEO or its policy of supporting same-sex domestic partners in the United States. We have achieved progress, because women as well as men can remotely pilot unmanned aerial drones to blow up heathen hospitals and weddings.

We learn the rules for sex-gender earlier than any other aspect of our personhood. Sex-gender is policed more vigilantly and personally assimilated more deeply than other forms of identity formation. Tell the average three-year-old boy he's a girl, or girl she's a boy, and prepare for a little blitzkrieg of tantrum and revolt. Sex-gender as a power structure is woven more tightly into the fabric of our lives, both public and private, than any other boundary. Sex-gender is more mystified by ideology, pop psychology, and pseudoscientific malarkey, more the bone of contention of increasingly arcane and impenetrable academic and theological debates, and more consequential in its implications for all of our other philosophical assumptions, than any other aspect of human sociality. That is why the twinned evils of patriarchy and woman-hatred (as well as their first cousin, homophobia[3])

3. An umbrella term to cover all forms of fear, disgust, and hatred directed at those

have proven to be the most difficult, persistent, and adaptable forms of social injustice to confront.

Two related notions in *Borderline*, in response to the arguments that women are now in the military and that women are now supporting war as public officials, are the "female decoy" and the "honorary male."

> In a plural society like the United States, male social power does not assign women one monolithic "script." Zillah Eisenstein has said that modern society restlessly "renegotiates" masculinity and femininity, often using what she calls "gender decoys"—individual women in power and individual women as spokespersons for enterprises that are still dominated by males and for males.
>
> . . . We can easily see that the corporate boardroom lacks females except to take the minutes and serve the coffee; but we don't typically think of the corporation and its boardroom as the product of the history of male dominance. This blind spot is maintained by *norm*-alization and gender-neutral liberal speech. We are then seduced by the argument that something called "equality" can efface history by putting more women on the board (as "gender decoys"). Shuffling the board may lead to small changes in its practices, but the function of the board is imbricated within the larger context of society and law. A few women in the boardroom does nothing that improves the lot of women generally, nor will they force the institution to adapt standpoints shared mostly by women. On the contrary, *women in power have consistently adapted to the existing masculinized culture*, where they serve as honorary males. This is why we need to read between the lines of gender-neutral speech.[4]

---

who—in various ways—fail to conform to what Adrienne Rich calls "compulsory heterosexuality." *Compulsory heterosexuality* does not mean someone is being forced into what we refer to as sexual orientation (a personal trait). Rich described sexuality as encompassing much more than the erotic. In particular she describes "lesbianism"—which she promotes—as women being women-identified, whether they have sexual relations with men or women or are sexually abstinent. In a system of compulsory heterosexuality, what are compulsory are the *roles*, where women see other women as competition for men, or where they favor their male children, or wherein men feel obliged to do all those "masculine" things that identify them as men. It goes to the division of men from women in support of sustaining men's power over women—in which we participate, willingly or not, through our many accommodations.

4. Goff, *Borderline*, 187, 210 (italics added).

The woman who becomes an "honorary male" is allowed to occupy a limited number of positions in the male world *provided she behaves like the men before her*. In doing so, she provides that ideological gender-cover without changing either the masculinized character[5] of the surrounding society or institution, without disrupting masculinity constructed as violence and conquest, and without changing any of the power structures that continue to exist (like racism, class power, and imperial crimes like wars and coups) in spite of minor sex-gender disruptions.

True story. When I taught at the United States Military Academy at West Point in the 1980s, around ten percent of the Corps of Cadets were female. West Point: male institution that fought against female inclusion until they were nearly forced at gunpoint. Masculine institutional character. In the cadet lingo of the day, anyone who did anything very well was called a "stud." He's a football stud. He's a chess stud. He's a PT (physical training) stud. Interestingly, when minority female cadets did things well, they were also called studs. She's a lacrosse stud. She's an academic stud. The women who were disliked were still called cunts and whores and dykes and whatnot—pretty standard misogynistic Army talk—but if a young woman managed to gain the respect of some of the men, by not rocking the boat and taking the sexist shit of cadets and faculty without complaint, her sign of acceptance was to become Storm Cat, the uber-ejaculate sire of many flat-racing thoroughbreds. She became an honorary male stud.

Move along.

Two bits of film criticism I'd included in *Borderline* to exemplify this idea were *GI Jane* and *Man on Fire*, a story about a woman who becomes an Honorary Man by becoming a gunfighter, and another story about a black guy who becomes an Honorary White Guy by becoming a gunfighter. Americans love gunfighters, and we love war. Our truest faith. When Charlie emailed me with his suggestion that we do more and smaller gendered-power books, Sherry and I had embarked on the long journey through five seasons of *Game of Thrones*—an often-pornographic, quasi-medieval, fantasy television series that could keep sex-gender analysis folks and sexual psychoanalysts busy for the next two centuries. It was

5. Not calling masculinity an *essence* of some kind, like a Great Penile Spirit that takes possession of people. Masculine means that constellation of characteristics that men-in-power are expected to exhibit, emulate, and/or hold in high esteem: aggression, lack of "emotionalism," toughness, the desire to conquer. Men were associated with power, power associated with these characteristics, and those characteristic were then separated out by social norms as the province of men.

this confluence of events, then, that gave me the idea of taking nine well-known films, released over a period of forty years, from *Star Wars* to *Jane Got a Gun*, in which there were well-recognized, strong female leads, and putting each of them under this particular gender microscope. Honorary males and gender decoys.

It was bell hooks, introduced to me by my sister many years ago, who convinced me of the value of cultural criticism. Again and again bell hooks has shown how popular culture, especially television and film, reproduces power structures. But she has also shown how critical engagement with popular culture is a pedagogical method that can reach a lot of people, meet them on familiar ground, and lead them through a process of defamiliarization that allows them to look past the mystifications of power that are written into these stories.

I doubt I can get many people to read sociological surveys; but I'm pretty sure a lot of people have seen the films included in this book. Also, if you are really intrigued by the way gender analysis unpacks into a complex architecture of heterodox insights, you can save up fifty dollars and buy *Borderline*.

Acknowledgments

PEOPLE SELDOM IMAGINE WHERE a writer actually works, or how. I work in the basement, right under an I-beam that supports the whole house, glancing occasionally out 8 x 24-inch windows at the sky and some treetops. I work on a computer table that I made out of forklift pallets. When I'm working, Sherry is somewhere nearby. She's been somewhere nearby for over a quarter of a century, and I wouldn't be writing this had she not been. In addition to all the caring work she contributes to this household, to our family, and to others in charitable endeavors, she contributes energy, humor, and creativity to our lives, and she has taught me more than she can ever know. She has always had my back, as I hope I have hers. We've watched a lot of movies together, too.

At 67, I've become a full-fledged Facebooker; and say what you will about all the potential problems with online interactions, the virtual friendships I share on this *bricoleur*'s medium are something I cherish from here in the outback of the deindustrializing Midwest. From here in our basement, I've been the beneficiary of dozens and dozens of compassionate, smart, committed, and knowledgeable people, especially of some extremely smart women. It would take three pages to name them all; so . . . you know who you are. Thank you.

Rebecca Bratten Weiss has my special gratitude for reading parts of this and providing essential feedback when she was not battling reactionaries in the Tibershpere. Charlie Collier, again, gets a thank you for being my advocate and liaison with Wipf and Stock.

And to all my kin, here and scattered hither and yon, again too numerous to count: without you, I am nothing.

Introduction

Human beings are storied creatures. No other creature tells stories. No other creature is formed by stories the way we are. An old English literature professor told me once that the most engaging stories always dealt with four things: love, death, sex, and power. I don't know if that's altogether true, but I'd be hard pressed to name the exception in my own reading, including the Bible.

As a Christian, who is hopefully being formed by a story—the one told in the Gospels—I'd point out that all these elements are in our story; but this seems a truism when you consider that our lives inevitably contain these four phenomena as well, all mixed up in a kind of magic mushroom psychodrama smoothie. It's making sense of them that can be difficult and even, at times, painful. Stories give order to experience and relations, meanings that transcend all four elements individually and make them more than the obsessions that pop our strings and make us dance like drunken marionettes.

In 2000, I was offered very well-paid temporary employment by Warner Brothers and Director Andy Davis (*The Perfect Murder*, *The Fugitive*) to serve as a military technical advisor for an Arnold Schwarzenegger male-revenge-fantasy[1] film called *Collateral Damage*. I worked in Los Angeles as well as on location in and around Xalapa, Mexico, where I became familiar with the nuts and bolts operation of movie-making. This ruined things for me as a diehard cinophile, because, while I knew of course that someone was shooting every movie I saw, it became far more difficult to watch a film or TV show afterwards without the constant realization that dozens of people had been just off screen with trailer-truckloads of equipment, or

1. An extremely popular genre.

that the people who were in character and so "present" on screen quit crying or raging or making out or thinking deeply between takes and smoked cigarettes while they goofed off or sampled the lickies and chewies at the craft service tables. I can no longer watch without realizing how badly many scenes would come off without clever editing and the right background music, how the highly intelligent and deeply spiritual character on screen might actually be a narcissistic, superficial twit, or, conversely, how the person we loathe on screen might be—in real life—the sweetest human being you'd ever want to meet. It's harder now, in short, to forget that I am being carried along by these artistic manipulations.

Which puts me in a good position to do this cultural criticism, but in not so great a position when I just want to relax and enjoy a story. Now I want to ruin it for you, too. Sharing is caring.

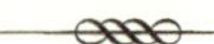

If there is one predominant theme from our most popular stories in modern cinema and television that divides it decisively from the story of the Gospels, it is the theme of *redemptive violence*. Walter Wink, in his essay "The Myth of Redemptive Violence," writes that

> The belief that violence "saves" is so successful because it doesn't seem to be mythic in the least. Violence simply appears to be the nature of things. It's what works. It seems inevitable, the last and, often, the first resort in conflicts. If a god is what you turn to when all else fails, violence certainly functions as a god. What people overlook, then, is the religious character of violence. It demands from its devotees an absolute obedience unto-death.[2]

Let's face it, when a storyteller wants to achieve dramatic tension, there is no cheaper, easier way than to set a hero against a villain, give the unredeemable villain the advantage long enough to build up the anger and anxiety of the audience, then turn the tables and cathartically rip apart the villain. In a sense, the hateful *object* is fungible (hate itself being indispensable) whether that hateful object is a serial killer or a lethal alien or an orc. That's the visceral payoff, that catharsis; but the rationalization that insulates *hatred* from critique is the conviction that violence redeems. Kill the villain, kiss the girl, and share lobotomy smiles with a glorious and infinite sunset. I grew up with this crap. You did, too.

2. Wink, *The Powers That Be*, 42.

More than merely relaxing, however, watching these stories is a form of rehearsal that leads us to seek out conflict and enemies in either imagination or reality. My late acquaintance through *Counterpunch*, Alexander Cockburn, in writing *about* writing about activist politics, asked the question: "Is your hate pure?" We still see even a critical and redemptive politics as decisively warlike, requiring an enemy to make ultimate sense, with hatred to fuel the resistance.

The theme of redemption through violence does not work for Christians, of course, because Jesus repeatedly emphasizes that his (and our) mission is to save *sinners*, who are sometimes villains, ourselves included. We redeem the prodigal son, the adulterous woman, the reviled tax collector, and not by shooting them with a gun. Anyone who knows my past and wants to know "why Christian?" just needs to read that part about "I came for sinners." Reprobates gladly accepted. I've been the villain. Thank you for not ripping me apart. I'm glad your hate was impure.

For a film protagonist to redeem the world with violence, the essential humanity of the villain has to be stripped away. The villain must be a monster (literal or figurative) or a devil (literal or figurative), or else that Bible we occasionally thump in other people's direction might jump up and smack us between the running lights with all that repentance and forgiveness stuff.

Wink gender-qualifies his claim:

> The myth of redemptive violence is the simplest, laziest, most exciting, uncomplicated, irrational, and primitive depiction of evil the world has ever known. Furthermore, its orientation toward evil is one into which virtually all modern children (boys especially) are socialized in the process of maturation.[3]

"Boys especially." Well.

Those who wield redemption through violence in film have historically been men. In the 1930s, it was *Captain Courageous*, *Stagecoach*, and *Tarzan the Ape Man*. In the 1940s, *The Maltese Falcon*, *The Big Sleep*, and *The Ox-Bow Incident*. In the 1950s, the Cold War Western reached new heights, including *High Noon*, *Shane*, and *Rio Bravo*. 1960s: *Spartacus*, *The Good, the Bad, and the Ugly*, and *The Magnificent Seven*. Oh yeah, they were also all *white* men, *The Magnificent Seven* excepted. Hollywood was American, after all. White men—the tough husband, father, or brother

3. Wink, *The Powers that Be*, 53.

figure—were responsible for white America's order. In the absence of their benign authority, there would have been chaos. They were often literally "manning" the boundary between "civilization" and "savagery."

Then along came the subversions of respectability and easy answers in *noir* fiction. Broken protagonists and ambiguously evil antagonists, along with a healthy helping of class criticism. Archetypical masculinity even in this subversion, however, retained above all the willingness to do violence. Take away everything else, but not my identification with being a Really Real Testicular Dude. Dashiell Hammett, where are you? Raymond Chandler?

The virtue of that manly violence was directly proportional to the viciousness of the vanquished villains; though as masculinity experienced further destabilizations, for example after the US defeat in Vietnam when the national masculinity was called into question, "virtuous violence," reluctantly delivered, received less and less cinematic attention than the plain macho willingness to do violence. This *willingness*—apart from context—became *the* masculine virtue, giving us the male-revenge-fantasy genre embodied in *Death Wish* and the displacement of taciturn Gary Cooper-like, seemingly-reluctant, redemptive violence by the mouthy, cruelty-celebrating, proto-fascism of *Dirty Harry* with his Really Big Gun.[4]

In the 1970s, even in the wake of the black freedom movement's advances, Hollywood stayed so white you could go snowblind: *The Godfather*, *Deer Hunter*, *Deliverance*. But white women, at least (directed by white men, of course) got in on the fatal-phallic action by shooting bad guys and monsters in *Star Wars* (1977) and *Alien* (1979), two films that spawned sequels throughout the 1980s, as Princess Leia and Ellen Ripley took up their weaponized penises and serially blasted their way to redemption in a new iconography—the Hot Chick with a Gun.

This is where we will pick up the history, with *Star Wars* and *Alien*; then we will work through seven more films and series featuring women who are touted as feminist icons (with one pedagogical exception, *Michael Clayton*) because they replace what were formerly men as the kinds of might-makes-right characters who variously get tough, kill, and conquer: *Silence of the Lambs* (1991), with Clarice Starling; *GI Jane* (1997), with Jordan O'Neil; *28 Days Later* (2002), with Selena; *Michael Clayton* (2007),

4. Never doubt for a moment, by the way, that guns in cinema and television *are* phallic symbols, weaponized phalli, even when they are wielded by women (who become for one shining moment, fatal-phallus in hand, Honorary Men).

with Karen Crowder; *The Girl with the Dragon Tattoo* (2011), with Lisbeth Salander; *The Hunger Games* (2012), with Katniss Everdeen; and *Jane Got a Gun* (2016), with Jane Hammond. We'll have it all: science fiction war, science-fiction monster, police procedural, military coming-of-age, zombie apocalypse, legal thriller, dystopian survivalist, and even a Western.

I would ask readers to ask these kinds of questions of each film. Of what class is the protagonist? What is the set-up for her story? What is the theme of the film? Who wrote the story? Who directed it? What is the worldview of the writer and/or director? What film conventions and tropes are employed in the story? How does our heroine prove herself? How does she adapt to male culture? Who is she attracted to, and who is attracted to her? What is her "special power," if any? What hooks us into the story and the character? What are the gender critiques that can be brought to bear on story and character? How can they be related to each other? What has changed as evidenced by this production, and what has remained? What has changed about gender as a power structure since the years covered in these productions?

Feminism is a contested term, and as a male I am reluctant to call myself feminist, though very sympathetic with a great deal of what many feminists say, because . . . well, they're most often right.

Feminism is a movement. Within it, like all social movements, there is controversy between various advocates from multiple standpoints and philosophical orientations. Most *people* are most *familiar* with the feminism that is amplified by mass media, because mass media streams its crap into our heads for countless hours. Mass media reacts to culture, then it selectively amplifies aspects of culture, and thereby reshapes culture. And what mass media *markets*, in response to "market forces," is primarily a version of feminism that will not overly discomfit the existing dominant class, will not criticize nationalism or capitalism, and does not confront the twin deities of militarism and violence. This gender-only feminism is *liberal* feminism. *There are several more kinds*, which is a key takeaway for readers as we step out on this critical journey.

The criticism of liberal feminism among conservatives, and among conservative Christians, is essentially *patriarchal*; that is, the criticism is self-consciously committed to the preservation of a male-over-female hierarchy. Mom is nurturing and obedient, happily servile, and sexually available to Dad, who is a benevolent dictator.

Our critique here of *liberal* feminism is quite different, because it doesn't want to rein in women's emancipation from patriarchal structures, but to dramatically *expand* women's emancipation as the essential basis of a much broader form of social emancipation. For many Christians, Christian feminists, non-Christian feminists, womanists, and secular radical feminist allies, what differentiates them (and I include myself here) from liberalism is liberalism's me-first individualism. On the subject of alternatives for collective solutions, there are some metaphysical and political variances; but with regard to individualism versus sociality, all these categories oppose liberalism by emphasizing sociality. All, as they may otherwise disagree, also criticize the liberal political fiction called "economic man" or "rational man," degendered-in-name as "economic *individual*" or "rational *individual*."

Just to clarify what we mean by liberal: *conservative* and *liberal* in popular speech, recognizable to even the politically incurious, represents two competing trends *within* the larger philosophical *tradition* of liberalism. So when we say liberalism here, we mean this to represent what both "conservatives" and "liberals" share in their beliefs. This polarity has confused many people unfamiliar with the wide body of feminist thought into believing that these two sides—conservative and liberal—constitute the whole range of argument about sex-gender and the feminist movement. There are Fords and Chevys. *Nada mas.*

Not so. Everyone from Thomists to Marxists to eco-feminists to Third-World and postcolonial feminists to womanists and postmodernists have criticized the *liberalism*[5] of liberal feminism; and none is obliged to

5. Okay, this one needs constant clarification. Liberal here does not mean the liberal of liberal/conservative a la Ford/Chevy. History has a strange sense of humor with language. Liberal here, as opposed to liberal in liberal-conservative in the preceding paragraph, refers to a political-philosophical tradition that can be traced back to some seventeenth century white fellas, like John Locke and Thomas Hobbes. Their basic framework that advocated representative government, individualism, and capitalist economics is shared by both modern day "liberals" and "conservatives," though it comes under fire not just from the above-named critics, but from many influential Christian philosophers as well. The tricky part, with regard to liberal feminism and liberalism more generally, is that the political rights advocated—like freedom of the press, as just one example—create a *formal* equality that ignores the *actual* inequalities that exist prior to the operation of the law. A rich person can deploy a far more effective press than a poor person. "Freedom of the press applies to those who own one." Or in Anatole France's explanation, "The law, in its majestic equality, forbids rich as well as poor from begging in the streets, sleeping under bridges, and stealing bread."

leave off the *standpoints* of women[6] that constitute the shared basis of all feminisms. The essence of this shared critique is what this book is about, but from the complicating standpoint of a Christian, and one who is white and male and Southern and old, for what all that's worth.

Masculinity and femininity are constructions that exist across from one another. Like right needs left to mean anything, like up needs down. The unity of opposites. Masculinity needs femininity and vice versa to define itself as *opposite*: up is the opposite of down, masculinity is the opposite of femininity.

Given the transhistorical identification of men with war, and war with security, and security with community virtue, and the organization of political communities around war-making, in addition to other gendered divisions of labor between men and women—and the exclusion and devaluation of those sexual minorities who are neither "masculine" males nor "feminine" females, and therefore disrupt the sex-gender symbolic order—*masculinity* has come to be identified as *aggressive, competitive, and instrumental*, whereas *femininity* is understood as *passive, cooperative, and expressive*.[7] In fact, every human being has the capacity for all six of these traits, and in each case, there are situations in which each trait is probably most appropriate. These are not inborn sexual traits, but *socialized* traits; and the division into masculine and feminine is culturally trained and policed until it is personally internalized.

Broadly speaking, by the time people are toddlers, we have pretty substantially internalized the expectations of masculinity or femininity; and by the time we are grown, we are completely habituated to them. So a great many men end up *becoming* more aggressive, competitive, and instrumental, and a great many women end up *becoming* passive, cooperative, and expressive from constant practice. We all want to fit in. And we are all living into some story or another that is already gendered. That's why movies. In this book. Because they are stories.

Men and women who fall short of these expectations are made to feel inadequate, as if they are somehow failures. And on the other hand, culture rewards conformity, and those who fit are rewarded and reinforced in their gender conformities, so we are often compelled—without realizing

6. Standpoint is crucial, because a man and a woman in exactly the same physical circumstances are experiencing very different things, with many of those differences related to having lived their lives as male or female bodies upon which culture writes very different stories.

7. Stets and Burke, "Femininity/Masculinity.

it—to *prove* our masculinity or femininity. Men are culturally formed to "need" to demonstrate aggression and strength (or to admire and valorize it in others). Men who don't are punished. Women are formed to "need" to aim at attracting men and competing with other women for the attention, approval, and sponsorship of men. Women who don't are punished. This makes it easy to *naturalize* these traits—to experience them so viscerally that they feel like the laws of *nature*.[8]

The problem for Christians who take the Gospel story seriously is that Jesus is pretty gender subversive. He is not competitive and instrumental. He is not unemotional. He is often passive and cooperative. He refuses to kill and *submits* to the cross. So while Christians can and should be extremely sympathetic with many feminist critiques, and while we understand why women seeking their emancipation from oppressive structures and stereotypes want to reject this polarity, a truly Christian idea of virtue—for men *and* women—most closely accords with those traits associated with *femininity*. That doesn't mean we have to accept the categories masculine and feminine, and therefore *choose femininity*.

On the contrary, it means, first, we can reject these *categories* as natural and inevitable. This polarity is the ideological aspect of a power structure that is fundamentally unjust to women and sexual minorities. Men have long exercised power, and being an effective man often means being a vicious one, *because the exercise of power is so often the exercise of vices*.

It is an error to reactively advocate for more *femininity* as a balance against masculinity. We want to advocate for *nonviolence* and *love*, gender irrespective. Because for Christians, anatomy and sexuality are immaterial; our mission is to make God's work of compassion visible in the world. That's why some of us have an issue with Christians (men especially, but also some women) having such an outsized preoccupation with which people rub which parts together intimately, but precious little to say about all the ways that Jesus's exemplary selfless and sacrificial service is nowhere to be seen in approved, state-certified "heterosexual" unions when so much of what goes on in those unions has nothing to do with love and is often self-serving, instrumental, fetishizing, objectifying, abusive, and sometimes even violent.

Courage is a virtue for men *and* women; but if we are given a choice between killing-hero and dying-martyr, for example, *or even a bold*

8. This accounts for the sometimes violent discrimination against sexual minorities, who "queer" the standards, so to speak.

trickster,[9] all of which can require courage, then our faithfulness to the Gospel story is predicated on choosing the martyr or trickster ahead of the killing-hero. Our God is a vulnerable God, one who took on flesh and submitted to the cross.

And yet, given the injustice of the gendered order, of male supremacy, we have to be sensitive to the ways that vulnerability (up to *martyrdom*) as a virtue for women in cinema (and church) *reinforces* the masculine-feminine stereotypes for an audience who has already internalized it. And we should recognize how attractive the aggressive, competitive, and instrumental woman in film is to the vast majority of women who suffer under male hegemony and feel policed and cut off when they display—in situations where it is set up to be perfectly appropriate—aggression, competition, and instrumentality. How could women not feel a little celebratory at a female character that quits putting up with injustice? While the response may be subject to our criticisms, the reason for the response is understandable and points to the real suffering of real women in the real world.

This complication is why we included the late Andrea Dworkin's quote at the beginning of the book. This "radical" feminist recognized that those traits generally identified with men were identified with *men-in-power*, and that a few women achieving that kind of power does not address the injustices that inhere *in the exercise of that power*. Liberal feminism had fenced itself off within "gender inequality" in such a way that white affluent feminists could focus on the inequalities between them and white affluent men and confront that power without addressing the ways that gender is nested into class, race, and nationality as historically unjust power structures perpetuated in part by the ignorance and denial of privilege other than sex-gender. Some early American feminists argued forcefully about the "injustice" of the franchise being afforded to black men before white women, clearly stating their conviction that black men were inferior to white women because white women were white. Elizabeth Cady Stanton said, "What will we and our daughters suffer if these degraded black men are allowed to have the rights that would make them even worse than our Saxon fathers?"[10]

The liberal feminism that seeks a theoretically "meritocratic equality" between men and women,[11] *within the existing power structures* of

9. An underappreciated aspect of Jesus during his journeys.

10. Wein, "Getting the Joke of White Feminism," para. 8.

11. Jesus explicitly opposed meritocracy.

industry, finance, and the war-justified state—like all power that has been destabilized by historic change—can eventually be embraced by those in power as a buffer against any deeper critique or action. A few black people can have equality with most white people so long as they perform exactly like "respectable" white people. A few women can have equality with men so long as they do not disrupt the power structures established by men, the processes and procedures that support those structures, or the fundamental way of knowing that interprets and mystifies the role of power.

The violent masculinity that has underwritten the male exercise of power and which has become essential to male identity can remain intact, so long as we only allow a few women—like the person of color performing in ways that feel nonthreatening to white people is accepted as an honorary white person—to be accepted as honorary men. This way we can retain on a broader scale those same power structures without the danger of destabilization, while entertaining the masses with the imagination of equality through identification with a few real or fictional tokens.

The fissure in this whole construction—as the radical feminists have long pointed out—is sex. The tough female cop in the police procedural flick is a "strong female character" who nonetheless perpetuates the idea that the police are what "stand between civilization and savagery," instead of the far more morally ambiguous class/race realities of actual police and actual policing. And women who "kick some ass" in film and television will almost always manage to retain enough of their "femininity" to appeal to metropolitan male adolescents as sex objects. The problematic popular message for young women, which accompanies this narrative in entertainment media and advertising is: "You don't have to surrender your sex appeal to be a kickass grrrl."

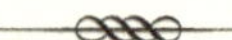

A quick historical overview explains the problem here.

Before feminism as a mass movement (the 1960s and 1970s to the present), and before several stages of industrialization/mechanization, masculinity and femininity were constructed in ways different from how they are constructed today. They still are in different places and cultures. But among Westerners, even as late as the early twentieth century, society was completely divided between male and female *spheres*. This division is what we call *structural gender* for the purpose of this book's analysis. It is not the same as our (biological) procreative status, which, with some few exceptions, is either male (XY, with sperm-producing testes and that little pollination probe) or female (XX, with fallopian tubes, eggs, and a womb).

Structural gender is a set of customs and social norms that divide speech, mannerisms, clothing, practices, attitudes, tools, and power into one masculine sphere—which men are expected to inhabit—and one feminine sphere—which women are expected to inhabit. This *attaches to* a biological procreative status, but it is *culturally*, not biologically, determined by it. The *biologically* female body is culturally marked within these structures.

Gender is a set of social constructions, though it is important to say that as we internalize these constructions—trained almost from birth—the only separation between the physical sex of a person and these constructions is analytical. The cultural and the physical always interpenetrate one another, each altering and remaking the other.

At one point, these separations were so strict and thoroughgoing that very few people questioned them. But with rapid changes in technology and economy, sometimes during the nineteenth and more often in the twentieth century, women were, by economic necessity more often than not, impressed into the same work forces as men, in factories at first,[12] then later in office spaces with computers. Men and women were suddenly using the *same* tools, and being formed by the *same* work; and this was very destabilizing of the gender order. Men grew to fear that with the erosion of these social boundaries, they would lose their place, their gender identity, and their power. They experienced a kind of sexual vertigo.

During periods of gender destabilization, there is always a social backlash, and if that fails to re-establish the old gender order, a new one is—as Zillah Eisenstein said—"renegotiated" to set male social power back on a new and firmer footing. As women have increasingly made incursions into formerly male terrain, gender has been forced off its footing in many tools, spaces, and work,[13] and it has been correspondingly amplified in the realm of *sexuality* proper: in our shared constructions of male and female sexual attraction, and in the manifold ways that sexual desire is triggered and maintained. If we both work in a cubicle with a computer, at least I—the man—can prove my male *bona fides* by ramping up my objectification of you—the woman. This is—pardon my *français*—what we can refer to as the

12. Dublin, "Women and the Industrial Revolution." For a time in the nineteenth century, women and children were massively impressed into factory labor.

13. Don't over-read this. A quick look at most construction crews, for example, will reveal how few women have entered into that domain.

"fuckability" factor. I can put every woman I see on a fuckability scale from one to ten, and thereby redefine and recapture women who have in other respects "invaded" the male sphere. Puts her back in her place.

This is a historically simplified account that ought to include the shift from the patriarchal male power of the feudal period to the *fraternal* male power of the modern period. Instead of one man—a father or brother or husband—controlling a woman, she has become the potential property, submissive partner (or victim) of every man, and so has frequently felt compelled to accept the control of one (husband) as protection against the rest (of men).[14]

This account should also include the so-called sexual revolution inaugurated by more and more effective means of birth control and by an ever greater cultural openness to non-marital sex. As some feminists will tell you, this was good news and bad news; because, while women were perfectly happy to have the sexual aspect of their beings validated and to relinquish it from strict male control, the response of males—even most of the radical movement males—had been to celebrate what they saw as *freer access to women's still-objectified bodies*—to which they *still* felt entitled . . . well, because they were men.

Between this passage from *paternal* male power to *fraternal* male power, the erosion of gendered space apart from sex, and the sexual revolution—which ended up heaping new expectations on women—gender, then, has been increasingly *sexualized.*

Most men now will theoretically accept women as doctors and lawyers and cops and soldiers—some of them—but women continue to be judged based on whether they are sexually attractive by male standards. As a male, I can grudgingly accept women in new kinds of work, but I reserve the right to sexually objectify her and pass judgement on her intrinsic value based on her "fuckability."

When we study the films in this book, we will find that most of the writers and directors are still men, and we will look for this particular "male gaze," that objectifying point of view that says you can be a woman with a gun or sword or archer's bow, but you have to be "hot." You have to be "fuckable." And this gaze is not any less male when a few women writers and directors do it, because we are all indoctrinated into these norms, women and men alike. Women, young and old, continue to judge *themselves* and

14. Pateman, *The Sexual Contract*, 154–88.

accommodate *themselves* to the "male gaze."[15] Women who succeed in the "hotness" competition are rewarded for that success, and can become its advocates. And so an ultra-rich actor like Cameron Diaz will say things like, "I think every woman does want to be objectified,"[16] assuming all women have her privilege, and that no woman's objectification (and her fuckability score) has led to her devaluation, humiliation, and abuse—including rape. Or that being "hot" qualifies a woman as a "valuable enough" human being, which leaves the overwhelming majority of women who fail to meet improbable, media-generated, media-hyped beauty standards being undervalued.

One thing that our characters have in common in the films we study in this book, to one degree or another, is that they are all, with a couple of qualified exceptions, portrayed as simultaneously tough and sexually appealing *by contemporary male standards.* If they were unattractive, then the stories themselves would be about "coping with unattractiveness," and our heroine would undergo The Makeover that would make her smile and everyone else go goggle-eyed at her transformation to beauty. The Makeover is a film *trope*,[17] a device or convention that is used again and again—because it makes money for filmmakers.

We will look at a lot of tropes in this book. Tropes about women in film are variously and humorously named things like the Smurfette Principle, the Disposable Woman, the Damsel in Distress, Hot Chick with Gun, Women as Background, Straw Feminist, Demon Seductress, Mystical Pregnancy, Women in Refrigerators, Manic Pixie Dream Girl, Take off Your Clothes, Mama Bear, Real Women Don't Wear Dresses, Romantic Rape, Young Chick Old Dude, Woman in Jeopardy, Pretty Women Live,

15. Mulvey, "Visual Pleasure and Narrative Cinema." The "male gaze" was a concept first articulated by British film theorist Laura Mulvey in 1975. Mulvey noted at the time (and it is still largely true) that writers, producers, and directors of film are overwhelmingly male. They are possessed of the sensibilities of males constructed by male-dominant cultures, including patriarchal notions about women, and they vacillate between sexually objectifying women, making atypical women monstrous and terrifying, or making women who are neither invisible and/or disposable. Men enjoy "looking" at women, voyeuristically, as a form of possession and power. The Freudian term for this is scopophilia. Mulvey showed how often male filmmakers transferred their own particularly possessive and "male" gaze into the point of view of the camera. What makes this problematic, as some female writers, producers, and directors come on board, is that women—internalizing the point of view of power—are often "gazing" at themselves and others through the psychological point of view of men, a kind of "double consciousness."

16. Huffington Post, "Cameron Diaz."

17. A film trope is a plot device used frequently enough to be recognizable as a kind of cliché.

and many others.[18] These tropes provide culturally recognizable handles for taking hold of the symbolic mechanics of filmmaking, and thereby a window into the thinking of (mostly male) filmmakers and directors, as well as their dog-trained audience (us).

And again, by giving the reader a look inside the mechanics, I'll probably ruin it for everyone. Before that, I would like to suggest (only suggest) a way for persons and groups to read this book. Through trial and error, groups can refine this process to get the most out of it. When you get to a chapter, *before you read it*, watch the film, but do not discuss it. Then read the chapter and take notes if you are inclined that way. Wait at least a full day and night before you watch the film again. If you are participating in a reading group, find a good discussion facilitator who keeps order, *prevents interruption and domination of the group by more forceful personalities*,[19] and who can keep track of the discussion threads (this is very important to all reading groups). Rinse and repeat. Discussion threads need not adhere strictly to the topic of the film.

Let a thousand flowers bloom.

I strongly encourage young people's participation, because one of the rationales for this book is that media becomes less a tool for propaganda and more a tool for purposeful social engagement when it is viewed critically. Who knows which young person in your group is tomorrow's bell hooks, Edward Said, Julie Bindel, Stanley Crouch, Jennifer Baumgardner, Ivan Illich, Elaine Showalter, or Cornell West?

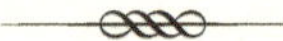

Let's go to the movies.

18. We won't see all of these, but several.

19. These are almost always men.

1

Perky Princesses and Lovable Rogues: Princess Leia

In 1977, George Lucas's film *Star Wars* became the highest-grossing film in history, a position it held for five years. War films, almost without exception, are exciting, and this one had "Wars" in the title. We went to see it expecting that adrenaline buzz. Based vaguely on Akira Kurosawa's *The Hidden Fortress*,[1] the film was about heroes using redemptive violence against villains.

Displaced from premodern Japan into an intergalactic mélange of tribal confederations—governed apart from the bad Empire by a Senate comprised of aristocrats—that are curiously technologically advanced enough for light-speed space travel and yet organized according to archaic social standards, Lucas substituted Jedi warriors for Samurai and light sabers for sword and staff.

Anything that makes that much money just has to be reproduced, and the *Star Wars* franchise has given birth to twelve puppies, as of this writing—so, thirteen films in total. Princess Leia, played by the late Carrie Fisher, appeared in six of them.

Let's start with, she was a princess. A princess. I have granddaughters, and when every one of them turns on a television or gets roped into a new kid movie by sales campaigns aimed at little girls, they are given princesses as role models. They can be "spunky princesses"—like Princess Leia—but they are also hyper-fem in appearance. Because a princess is pretty. And a princess, at least as far as I know my history, is part of a hereditary aristocracy. We like hereditary aristocracies, even though we celebrate their undoing in grammar-school history classes where we

1. Barber, "The film Star Wars stole from."

break away from the wicked King George. We like hereditary aristocracies in *Star Wars*. We like them in *Lord of the Rings*. We like them in *Game of Thrones*. We miss that sense of Platonic order.

Where do we meet Princess Leia Organa of Alderaan? Being captured as a rebel spy by the dastardly Darth Vader. A few (spunky) retorts to Vader, and she disappears. She reappears in a holographic message to our humble hero-to-be, Luke Skywalker (who, it will be revealed, is possessed of Jedi superpowers and specially chosen because he is, unknowingly, part of the hereditary aristocracy and Leia's sibling). Leia is the Damsel in Distress, a pretty woman whose required rescue will give the male protagonist an opportunity to prove his mettle in a lethal-force rescue op.

That's the set-up. So far so good.

Leia does a few things that break patterns. She stands up (spunky princess style) to her degenerately brilliant captor, Darth Vader, instead of squealing helplessly and getting the vapors. She smart-mouths Governor Tarkin, her captor's boss. Luke and his new friends, Hans Solo and his primate companion Chewbacca, stage the lethal-force rescue op, mowing down imperial troopers by the dozens between bug-eyed panting and humorous quips. Leia does not swoon into the rescuers arms or have to be led out by the hand, raining tears and breaking the china with high-pitched screams. She gets a gun (a blaster) and "gets some," taking out her fair share of robotically-Nazified storm troopers who all need serious remedial marksmanship training, because they can't hit a barn door.

Apart from Leia, in the first film there are no female characters, unless you count some alien hookers in the bar and a throwaway aunt in Luke's desert home with six short lines. In fact, in the *Star Wars Trilogy*, if you subtract Leia, the total time other women spend speaking on screen is sixty-three seconds. In three movies.

Katha Pollitt named this trope "the Smurfette Principle."

> Contemporary shows are either essentially all-male, like "Garfield," or are organized on what I call the Smurfette principle: a group of male buddies will be accented by a lone female, stereotypically defined . . . The message is clear. Boys are the norm, girls the variation; boys are central, girls peripheral; boys are individuals, girls types. Boys define the group, its story and its code of values. Girls exist only in relation to boys.[2]

2. Pollitt, "The Smurfette Principle."

So while Leia doesn't fit perfectly into this principle, because she is the still-pretty honorary male, she is uncomfortably close to being Smurfette in the larger scheme of the *Star Wars* franchise. And as we can see in this film series, written and directed by rich white men, this is a boy story from beginning to end. When women show up, these writer-director-dudes interpret a feminist sensibility as representing one woman as honorary male, sufficiently attractive to Average Adolescent Boy.

Carrie Fisher was ordered onto a "fat farm" by producers to lose ten pounds before the boys club would allow her on screen. Before Episode VII, Fisher was ordered back to the "fat farm," whereupon she self-deprecatingly quipped, "They only want to hire three-quarters of me."[3]

Hot Chick with a Gun trope. A gunslinging woman is not women's emancipation. Sorry. Just no. This trope has gone much further than Leia, as we can now see the "calendar girl" posed in lingerie with porn makeup on a Harley cradling her AR-15. It happens. The Hot Chick with a Gun trope is just the exoticization of women into a "sexy beast," the eventual conquest of which is super-extra-probative of some steroidal gym-bodied, bigger-gun-wielding stud. The point here, though, is that Leia is only allowed on the show because she is "attractive," and only allowed to do man-stuff like kill folks while making smart-assed remarks if she retains the capacity to make boys snicker and say, "I'd do her." This is how she retains her femininity—which has been sexualized as she "invades" common spaces with men. How do girls internalize this? "You can kick ass and still be hot, still feminine." Nothing to see here, move along.

Who is Leia going to be attractive for? Next trope please. The Loveable Rogue. Hans Solo. Because boys who are courteous, gentle, and considerate are just boring as hell and they don't get a girl's juices flowing like a macho bad-boy. If someone can find me a more hackneyed trope in film and television than the Loveable Rogue, email me. Now, in a PG-rated film like *Star Wars* that gets half its market share from boys of acne-fighting age, the Loveable Rogue is a selfish prick, who occasionally shows signs of redeemability by doing something nice for someone helpless, and he never kills innocents (because his marksmanship is always perfect, unlike those wall-eyed Imperial Storm Troopers), and he's loyal as hell to his real friends, or friend—in this case, an Ape-Man who always makes the exact same noise, like a vacuum cleaner that just sucked up a shoelace, which our hero can instantly interpret into a paragraph of detailed

3. Herman, "Mothers of the Rebellion."

technical information. Leia's job is to confront the Loveable Rogue Hans (spunkily) until they are suddenly drawn into pheromone range, whereupon the Loveable Rogue molecules penetrate her blood-brain barrier and overwhelm her with the urge to mate.[4]

Leia's desirability is chaste, for the most part. This is PG-land. She is cute, virginal, not yet despoiled in the fantasies of that boy in the audience, who will someday be her Hans and wipe her hard drive with his loveable bad-boy mojo. In case we fail to realize how desirable she is, though, once George Lucas prevailed upon Fisher to sufficiently slim down, he made sure that in *The Empire Strikes Back*, in a scene reminiscent of Orientalist tales like *Desert Song*, Leia is held captive among other sex slaves—though she is not yet despoiled—by Jabba the Hut, the bloated urchin with a profanely phallic tongue, and she is displayed for the audience in a provocative semi-reclined position wearing a golden bikini.

This is "male gaze" country, folks. The director has it; and he is passing it along to you. This is the seizure of the objectified female body by the male eye-beam. Jabba the craven oriental despot with Leia the sex slave is a white fantasy, too, that turns on the transgression of the virgin and transformation into whore, eroticizing female humiliation. The Damsel is again in Distress—yeah, we know that one—and the boys get to see Leia undressed. The girls learn . . . that boys like to see them undressed.

She can be an honorary male—gun-toting and smart-mouthing—but she has to be hot and susceptible to Hans's masculine bad-boy sex mojo. Gender . . . sexualized. Men . . . interpreting feminism to the greatest male advantage. Equality . . . when women become more like men.

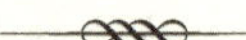

4. It's all just good, clean fun, except that we are storied creatures—male and female and in between—and we adapt our actions and attitudes—often without any cognitive intervention—to live into the stories we know. Real boys try to be loveable rogues, until they go R-Rated and try to be full-blown assholes—the Anti-Hero who is damaged from his manly experience; and real girls learn that this is desirable, that it is their job to accentuate the loveable and mitigate the rogue. We learn sociality, including desire, through *mimesis*, by emulating role models. Mimesis is a form of learning that is deeply embodied, because it is practical. We do mimesis with our bodies. "Sexual desire is awakened and developed in mimetic processes. There, sexual difference is experienced, and sexual identity is learned and acquired" (Goff, *Borderline*, 82). Sexual desire, for men and women, is not simply "natural." It is learned. That's why fat people, e.g., might be considered desirable in one culture and devalued in another. In heterosexual relations, we teach young men to be unpleasant, and we teach young women to eroticize that. This is a set-up for abuse.

The *Star Wars* franchise did, after thirty years, discover non-white people and a few more women. By the time Rey shows up in *The Force Awakens*, they'd learned enough not to be as heavy-handed with the tough-girl-as-feminist (developed by a man), though the obligatory "hotness" remained. *Rogue One* pissed off the so-called alt-right (a neologism for modern American fascists), which means the movie can't be all bad, based on the fact that members of the alt-right want women to return to the status the blood-and-soil boys fantasize they had around 200 years ago.

Let's talk about the Lovable Rogue trope in a bit more depth. One of the attractions of the Lovable Rogue trope is the idea that, while our rogue has some ethical issues, he retains enough of a moral core to hint at his future redemption. One of the problems with this is that this redemption—when the Lovable Rogue is cast as a romantic interest—is only provoked by protectiveness of his own heterosexual love interest. It is a hugely successful trope, unlikely to die out any time soon. But there are several, far more troubling problems with this trope, and how it is entangled in questions about class, men, women, sex, desire, and power.

Hans Solo, like many Lovable Rogues, is a class-differentiated character. Leia is royalty, and her initial aversion to Solo's behavior is his lack of deference and a certain boorishness in his behavior. Encoded as class, this is still a gendered trope, because the working class, down-in-the-dirt male persona is at root a male corrective to female delicacy and decorum . . . even though Leia in particular will correct Hans's corrections by picking up a blaster when necessary. It's the flip side of a Pygmalion/Pretty Woman narrative, where the upper-class man converts the working-class woman into a princess (with whom he then falls in love).[5]

Meanwhile, back in the real world, where boys and girls are taking these tropes in and trying to apply them in their own, messier and more consequential lives, this reinforces the idea that—in the marketplace of casualized sex—girls like Bad Boys. Because "nice guys" are boring. This is actually a hotly debated, long-standing internet topic, so much so that in 2003 Geoffry Urbaniak and Peter Kilman published the results of a study of this debate,[6] subtitled "Do Nice Guys Really Finish Last?" The notion that all theoretical men are in a sexual competition for all theoretical women is assumed in the way the question is constructed. Here is the "shocking" abstract:

5. In *Overboard*, Kurt Russell's working-class male schools Goldie Hawn's pampered, rich female; and she eventually learns how to love being his servile and fecund housewife.

6. Urbaniak and Kilman, "Physical Attractiveness and the Nice Guy Paradox."

> The nice guy stereotype asserts that, although women often say that they wish to date kind, sensitive men, when actually given a choice, women will reject nice men in favor of men with other salient characteristics, such as physical attractiveness. To explore this stereotype, two studies were conducted. In Study 1, 48 college women were randomly assigned into experimental conditions in which they read a script that depicted 2 men competing for a date with a woman. The niceness of 1 target man's responses was manipulated across conditions. In Study 2, 194 college women were randomly assigned to conditions in which both the target man's responses and his physical attractiveness were manipulated. Overall results indicated that both niceness and physical attractiveness were positive factors in women's choices and desirability ratings of the target men. Niceness appeared to be the most salient factor when it came to desirability for more serious relationships, whereas physical attractiveness appeared more important in terms of desirability for more casual, sexual relationships.[7]

The sarcasm about "shocking" is not just that any eighteen year old could have told them this without a survey, but that this survey begins with the assumption that all women and all men can be adequately represented by a sample taken exclusively from 194 college-aged American women. Will any women who fall outside that category, and that mindset, please stand up. The authors even cite the "paradoxical" differences between their own survey and similar survey among "92 married couples." Well, butter my behind and tell me it's a biscuit! The majority of married couples respond differently to a survey than the majority of college students.

Meanwhile, without a survey to support an obvious conclusion, Melissa Fabello, writing for *Everyday Feminism*, asks and answers.

> Why do some of the women go for the assholes?
>
> Here's why: We're told to.[8]

Who told them to? Well, Cry-Baby Walker, Troy Dyer, Bender, Warrick Brown, Hans Solo, Tyler Durden, Stanley Kowalski, James Bond, Curtis Taylor, Bobby Axelrod: a whole raft of hot-boy vampires have been telling young women *what they ought to desire* for quite some time—men who, in any scenario apart from the canned one in which they appear in film, would be garden variety, ethically-challenged, me-first, arrogant asshats.

7. Ibid.

8. Fabello, "Breaking down the assumption."

And for anyone who *knows* that advertisers advertise and fashion companies change fashions because they know these desire-production gambits work, and who then *says* that the dynamics of sexual desire cannot be likewise influenced by mass media . . . well, you're going to have to sell that elsewhere.

Just as young men are influenced by film archetypes, so are young women. College-aged is dug right down into that demographic. Barely-formed, inexperienced, often well-protected, inundated with !!!SEX!!! from every side and in the sexual hothouse of college, confused, attention-seeking, and often with very few interpretive tools to help them navigate these new challenges, young people in the industrialized metropoles, by and large, *have spent their entire lives having perceptions and desires managed by big business and its media.* They have been indoctrinated into what is heterosexually desirable, and that indoctrination has been reinforced by peer relationships where these sex-gender norms of desire are as ruthlessly policed as a Cairo checkpoint.

As the pseudonymous Hugh Ristik blogs:

> Women's preferences in men are important both for the interests of men and for the interests of women, for at least the following reasons: (1) female preferences may be implicated in their complicity with gender oppression, (2) some men harm themselves and/or harm women in response to rejection by women, or widely disseminate misogynistic attitudes, (3) female preferences influence male behavior on both implicit and conscious levels, and (4) cultural discourse over female preferences influences the behavior of both men and women, specifically through constructions of masculinity that can become harmful to both men and women.[9]

And there, to coin a phrase, is the rub-a-dub.

For the record, "nice guys" is not—in terms of statistical analysis—operationalizable. If you visit the online debates over whether "nice guys finish last," the comments sections are filled with a not-so-nice whine-fest of commentary from the guys who "finished last." This usually means one or more women told them no, and it pissed them off—a lot.

So, below the surface, we have the eroticization of assholes, combined with the wounded sense of denied-entitlement that, in its extreme form may end up being a different kind of asshole . . . like Dylan Klebold maybe. Sometimes, when I read, study, and write this stuff, I despair of being male. I have to remind myself that internet comments sections are dominated by

9. Ristik (pseudonym), "Misunderstanding Patriarchy."

angry, neurotic men, and that most of us do not lurk there. So, Number 2 from Hugh Ristik? Caveat: saying that "some men harm themselves and/or harm women in response to rejection by women" should not be interpreted as women being responsible for twisted, sexually-terrified men. On the other hand, we have to acknowledge this relational reality, especially in a world where any form of restraint or prudence (think of potty training for adults, only with regard to sex) is anathema. I'll tell you one thing that hasn't changed since the bad old days of strict male authoritarianism and women trapped in men's whore/Madonna complexes: No matter how badly a misguided sexual relationship between a man and woman turns out, women more often than not still suffer the worst consequences. *Plus ça change, plus c'est la même chose.*

What is the similarity between a good-looking asshole and a frustrated "nice guy"? Both of them feel they are entitled to sex because they want it, and are therefore entitled to access to women's bodies. It reminds me of something a woman who was a political organizer from Utah once told me: "We are all different. To punish me, God made me heterosexual."

Rebecca Bratten Weiss gives us a bit of nuance on how this trope coaxes women into abusive spaces:

> The lovable rogue trope is very old, and it's effective because it taps into a very specific desire some women have, and some cultures encourage: to exert one's sensual powers to reform the Byronic bad boy. This is huge in nineteenth century novels, and continues to this day in erotic literature. Why women read novels like *Fifty Shades* (and others better written) is for the "taste of danger." He's bad, and he'll hurt you . . . which in life is terrifying, but in a story it can be either an imaginative foray into a species of eroticism, which is a whole nother moral issue . . . or a way of confronting our fears about sex and the predatory male.[10]

Rogues, in the real world, are often not only *not* lovable, they are frequently incapable of loving anyone but themselves, and they see your role as their sexual partner to be facilitating their own self-fulfillment. You see how many times "self" fits into that construct? Flip that coin, and when they don't feel fulfilled (whatever that means in their self-involved little minds), stand by. Movie tropes aside, the cause of that lack of fulfillment will be you, and then "*You* make *me* feel wonderful" becomes "*You* made *me* so angry I had to beat hell out of you."

Now, let's jump forward two years to another science fiction film.

10. Email exchange with the author.

2

"Here, Kitty, Kitty" and the Toothy Vagina: Ellen Ripley

IN 1979, THE PROLIFIC director-producer Ridley Scott won the Saturn Award for best Director and best Science Fiction drama for his breakthrough movie *Alien*. *Alien* was not an homage piece like the original *Star Wars*, not a PG version of Samurai Astronauts.

Most of us know the story itself. Fast forwarding through it . . . cargo space freighter diverts to planetoid to check out strange signal . . . a recon team checks out a bizarre-looking structure . . . one member of the team is facially impregnated with an alien being that is brought on board to terrorize the crew . . . crew fights briefly and ineffectually against killer alien until one crew member—second mate Ellen Ripley—becomes the lone survivor . . . well, along with a cat . . . Ripley sets the main ship to nuclear self-destruct, boards the "life raft" shuttle . . . escapes . . . final plot twist, the alien has slipped on board the "life raft," and Ripley finally—in one last tense scene—has to kill it. Boom. The end.

Alien was an R-rated sci-fi movie that opened, contra *Star Wars*, with the volume turned way down. It begins with a languid wake-up sequence, followed by a casual breakfast scene, and only after this low-key opening does the tense orchestra music background the action as the landing encounters trouble. The crew finds itself in a damaged craft on a howling, stormy, dark planet resembling a Hieronymus Bosch nocturne. Damage to the landing craft is not catastrophic, but they will be stuck on this inhospitable planet for seventeen hours to do repairs before they can return to the mother ship, who they call . . . well, "Mother."[1] Remember this when we come back to the psychoanalytic manipulations of this film.

1. Named *Nostromo*, after a charismatic shipping company employee in a Joseph

Meanwhile, let's go check out this strange signal.

The recon party enters an apparently crashed craft, whereupon Executive Officer Kane has an exoskeletal-scorpionic-crab-thing leap up and attach itself to his face through his space helmet. So the action begins. Thirty-five minutes into the movie, which in movie years can cover a decade. As I said, Scott takes his time in the build-up. From there, of course, it quickly ascends to the violent climax, resolution, and dénouement.

Sigourney Weaver plays Ripley, the lead. Warrant Officer Ripley—at first a minor character—begins to emerge with a humorous remark to a colleague to "fuck off," which posthaste carries Ripley far, far from Princess Leia territory and establishes her as a "modern" earth woman.

The recon team returns with Captain Dallas, Navigator Lambert, and the injured Kane. Ripley, now the senior person on board, comes into her own as a character by refusing entry to the angry Captain Dallas and to Lambert (the film's other woman character), who have hauled the unconscious and thing-colonized Kane back to the shuttle. So, yeah, Ripley is capable of making the tough decisions under pressure. This is the point at which many viewers begin to see Ripley as a potential badass.

Though she screams at least three times (I'd scream if confronted by that thing), she also demonstrates courage in the battle with the alien-monster and decisiveness in working through tactics to get away. Ripley ends up traipsing through the set, steely-eyed and sweat-streaked, with a flaming gun in her hand. In the final confrontation, she gets hold of something like a spear gun (what it is for on a space ship we can't say—stopping off in Belize for a dive on the way home?), with which she dispatches the monster and (in her androgynous idiom) "blows it to fuck out into space." Stern, tough-talking, decisive, willing to kick ass, and carrying phallic weapons. Feminist, right?

Ridley Scott is not now and has never been feminist in any meaningful sense of the term, though he knows how to profitably ride cultural waves. He is a filmmaker. He knows how to build dramatic tension. In this film, he also knows how to run a kind of psychoanalytic subtext that captures the audience's sexual subconscious at the same time they are cognitively fixed on the mechanics of the plot. This film is positively brimming with post-Freudian, quasi-Lacanian sexual symbolism that speaks not to *women's emancipation*, but to *male disorientation* in a high period of the feminist

---

Conrad novel who becomes obsessed by a shipment of silver he has stolen but can never use, and who is finally killed while attempting its recovery.

movement, with the trope of Monstrous Female alongside a heaping helping of manipulative, intentionally disorienting, sexual confusion.

> Most critiques, academic and otherwise, ultimately conclude that *Alien* is a feminist film because of its representation of the workplace as a home to equality and a place where traditional gender roles have been obliterated. But there's something else lingering under the surface: fear. Not the fear of the devouring *Alien*, but a fear and anxiety of a future where the equalizing of the sexes might lead to the blending of sexual biology as well. What is ultimately revealed by *Alien* is the anxiety of men.[2]

Even that single-word title, evocative of disorientation: *Alien*. Let's go back and watch this movie now from the beginning.

Barbara Creed's essay, "Horror and the Monstrous Feminine,"[3] begins with a little quote from the classic Hitchcock horror film *Psycho*: Norman Bates, saying simply, "Mother's not herself today." It's always Mother, isn't it? In Creed's book, entitled *The Monstrous Feminine*,[4] she describes the ways in which men have historically projected their weirdest fears onto women, how this projected fear has been expressed in male myths, and how those male myths, as well as their assimilation by males in societies up to the present, have been reworked as psychoanalytic theory . . . which has also been assimilated and, as an effect of its assimilation, then become self-fulfilling. (European bourgeois) Man constructs psychoanalysis; (male) psychoanalysis constructs man (and woman).

In short, men have blamed women for everything wrong for quite some time. Blame has been incorporated into our symbolic grammar and thereby into our precognitive consciousness. Creed relates her analysis of a number of horror films (*Alien* included in that genre) to the notion of *abjection*, developed by Julia Kristeva, a European psychoanalyst and philosopher. *Abjection*, not to wear readers out with the deeper exploration of this subtle and arcane idea, is anything that disturbs our symbolic boundaries, especially the boundaries between subject and object.

With Freud, Lacan, and other Western male psychoanalysts, the person/patient is the subject and everything outside it, including people, are objects for one thing or another, especially for the satisfaction of (often unrecognized) desires. Abjection throws us off, disorients us. Poo-poo and

2. Haggstrom, "Reassessing *Alien*."

3. Creed, "Horror and the Monstrous Feminine"

4. Creed, *The Monstrous Feminine*.

corpses and blood and such have this effect.[5] Women and mothers are ripe for this, especially among squeamish men, because . . . well, (whispers) menstruation. And childbirth. And changing shitty diapers. And nursing. And the conflicted feelings people all have about Mom, because in six thousand years of male-dominated society, every relation to Mom between her and her kids is a set-up for psychological confusion. So we both love and blame Mom, and we have all these conflicted *feelings* . . . especially boys. Because as soon as possible, we push boys to reject anything girl, and to dis-identify with the one person upon whom, in patriarchal society, we've depended in the very first and formative years of our lives. *Alien* pounced on this male insecurity like a cat on a cockroach.

Birth, as any of us know who have given it or been there while others do, might be surrounded by the shiny white aseptic walls and stainless steel of hospital chic, but the process itself is a wet, grunting, crying, sweaty, squirming, blood-watery mess.[6] Miraculous and awe-inspiringly, breathtakingly humbling, in my view, but not tidy or linear. And yet *Alien*'s opening scene is a birth scene, but an aseptic, bloodless, quiet birth scene. The spaceship is named "Mother," remember?

Seven nearly naked people, wearing only snowy-white diapers, lay in Snow White cells,[7] arranged like flower petals, deep in the "womb" of the ship after we've been carried by the steady-cam down a long (fallopian?) tube. A flicker. The lights go on. Psshhhhhh, the glass covers on the cells rise, Kane is the first to awaken, slowly, blinking at the light, rising languidly, feeling his limbs. Mother brings the crew to life (birth!). It's not just the boundary between male and female that will be *abjected* in this film. Again and again, it is the boundary between organic and technological.[8]

Suddenly, we are all sitting around a communal breakfast table, in what was for the 1979 audience a company breakroom. People are eating, joking, smoking cigarettes. One of the maintenance crew is lobbying for

5. The poo-poo was in me, now it's out of me . . . boundary issues. Blood? Inside-to-outside the skin boundary. Makes some folks faint. That corpse was alive, now the life abandoned it. Big, scary boundary issues.

6. A note to other Christians: When Jesus is pierced by the Centurion's spear, blood *and* water flow out of his side—the birthing of new life.

7. *Snow White* is a German fairy tale in which the protagonist—a good princess, of course—is put into a state of suspended animation by a bad step-mother.

8. Scott would revisit these two themes, sexual confusion between male and female, and confusion (also sexualized) between organism and machine, in *GI Jane* and *Blade Runner*, respectively.

more money when they deliver their payload of ore. We even have a minor labor dispute, settled by quoting the contract. Four men, two women, somewhat gender-neutralized by everyone using last names. One of the mechanics tosses a sexual crack about what he "wants to eat" at one of the women, Lambert, who grins demurely, simultaneously embarrassed and amused; but men and women are working together, so there is some kind of equality . . . right?

Creed reminds us of our psychoanalysis. The female body, the mother's body, is "both life and abyss."[9] "Mother" has rebirthed the crew, and now issued an order (to go into another abyss, which also turns out to be a giant womb). That's why suspended animation was suspended eleven months from home. "Go to this nearby small planet and check out an unknown signal." When they follow Mother's order, the shuttle craft is *released* from the mother ship by an attachment called "the umbilicus." No kidding.

When we first land, Ash the Science Officer reads out the atmosphere from his instruments. "Almost primordial," he says. There is that word, now sent along through the audience's pre-cognitive pathways, *primordial*. Mother. Umbilicus. Primordial. And so the members of the reconnaissance team—Captain Dallas, navigator Joan Lambert (whose character is emerging with the personality of a cigarette-sucking surly teen), and Executive Officer Kane—don their protective suits and venture out into a literal howling void. As they approach the source of the mysterious signal (mythical sirens?), we see what appears to be the canted tail of a crashed craft, raised and separated against the night sky like two opened legs. Before you say I'm reading into it, wait. The recon team approaches, and where do they enter the craft? Precisely at the crotch, and through an opening that appears uncannily like a vaginal orifice. Primordial . . . cue the spooky music.

Inside, there are structures, fractal and strangely indeterminate. Are they machine-like or organic? The space is engulfingly enormous, the Great Consuming Womb, within which our little space people with large round heads look—from a distance—okay, a lot like spermatozoa. The audience is entranced by the strangeness of it, unaware of how the creators are tapping those little pre-cognitive, mytho-psychoanalytic tuning forks. Our team encounters a vertical surface, just over head high. They climb over, and there it is . . . what is that? Again, a strangely mechanical, strangely organic structure that they somehow determine immediately to be a dead life form. The camera pulls back. Up close, it looked a bit like skeletons copulating in heating

9. Creed, *The Monstrous-Feminine*, 60.

ducts; but as we see the whole thing, it is a fifteen-foot phallus, ribbed, erect, and aiming thirty degrees above level. A penis completely enveloped by a cathedral-sized womb? Sexual confusion, anyone?

The artwork that inspired the set in *Alien* was adapted directly from that of H. R. Giger, at Scott's request. Giger specialized in sexually confusing artwork that was an intentional organic-mechanical mashup. Screenwriter Dan O'Bannon stated explicitly that *Alien* was designed to make men in the audience "cross their legs" with sexual insecurity, not in order to promote feminism but *to heighten the horror-effect*. And he and Scott agreed that Giger's highly sexualized biomechanical style was perfect for bringing this to life on the big screen.[10]

David Dietle, who researched the making of *Alien*, wrote, "None of the sexual imagery in Alien is unintentional. For example, in the picture above the human crew members are 'invading' the alien ship, so in effect those are man sized sperm crawling through it. From here, John Hurt's character, Kane, plumbs the depths of the ship's 'womb' to find an endless landscape of eggs." The men who made it were telling a symbolic story of male anxiety in the face of an increasingly influential feminist movement.[11]

Kane is taken back to the shuttle craft, and the egg he has fertilized as a sperm has now become a phallus rammed down his own throat (impregnating him, as it turns out).[12] The shuttle craft returns to the orbiting Mother. The thing appears to die and fall off, but at breakfast again the recovering Kane, in one of the most memorable scenes in the film, gives birth. That is, a little monstrosity that looks like a penis with a fanged vagina at its tip, tears bloodily out of his abdomen, killing him.[13]

During the hunt to kill the alien who has absconded to somewhere within the craft, the thing manages to grow to the size of well-fed, adult-boar polar bear, with a head that looks like a stainless steel inverted penis (pointing rearward) with a wetly dripping fanged vagina on the face, out of which can emerge another phallus with another fanged vagina, also dripping viscous fluids from the tip.

10. Dietel, "*Alien*: a Film Franchise Based Entirely on Rape."

11. Just two years later, when Scott released *Blade Runner*, his protagonist Rick, played by Harrison Ford, falls for a hyper-femme female cyborg, who he warms up for sex by slapping her around. And it really turns her on. This is Ridley Scott, the "feminist."

12. Men are often obsessed by the "special horror" of males being raped, ergo the plentitude of squirmingly uncomfortable prison-rape jokes.

13. The Latin psychoanalytic term for the toothy vagina, a notion that also appears in various myths, is *vagina dentata*.

As the old Haitian proverb goes, "beyond the fanged vagina is a fanged vagina."[14]

First, Captain Dallas goes looking, then disappears suddenly from their tracking device. Now Ripley is in charge, and she becomes really assertive. During the continuing search for the homicidal alien, mechanical engineer Brett goes searching for the ship's mascot-cat named Jones, calling "Here, kitty kitty." He is ambushed by the alien, and we get our first close look at that retractable pecker with the biting labia on the tip. Holy castration complex, boys!

"*Alien* reveals a frighteningly voracious sexuality," writes Rebecca Bell-Metereau.[15]

Later, Ripley will likewise be calling for Jones the cat, "Here, kitty kitty," whereupon she will also be confronted by the monster. *Here kitty kitty* echoes over, under, around, and through the combination of sexual disorientation and terror of the fanged vagina. The pussy has teeth.

Ripley confronts Ash, the Science Officer, after she tries to override the company command to bring the critter in for "their weapons program." Ash attacks Ripley with super-human strength, and a suspiciously semen-like sweat begins to ooze from his pores with the effort, telling the audience that he is himself not human (he's an android). He knocks Ripley out, then—in a weird and completely gratuitous way—instead of throttling her with his super-human strength, or just using any of the nearby blunt instruments to bludgeon her, he decides to kill her by rolling a wank-magazine into a surrogate phallus (in this scene, tellingly, there are nude pin-up girls plastered on the wall in the background) and cramming it down her throat in a kind of forced and nearly-fatal fellatio. Ripley, the tough woman, we can be reminded now, is still a woman, still a sex object, still subject to sexual humiliation (or sexualized assassination).

If that's not enough for us to figure it out, in a scene that is not even in the screenplay, Ripley, as lone survivor, has taken off in the shuttle and destroyed Mother (get it?). She then does a strip show for the boys in the audience, peeling off one after another layer until she is in a flimsy, nipple-accentuating tank top and bikini panties that have sagged enough to reveal the cleft of her buttocks. This is the Take Off Your Clothes film trope, a specific accommodation to the male gaze. Here, it is Ripley killing the Mother

14. Okay, I made that up, too. The real proverb is *deye mon gen mon*, meaning *beyond the mountain is a mountain.*

15. *Bell-Metereau, "Woman: The Other Alien in Alien."*

then making herself available—via cinematography—to us males and our grasping gazes. Or rather, here it is Ridley making Ripley available—via cinematography—to us *fellow* males and our grasping gazes.

Wait, we're not done yet. She discovers the alien is on board, apparently sleeping on a shelf. Penile-toothy-vaginal aliens get sleepy after they eat, too, it seems. The stripped down Ripley—no longer the tough leader, but a female body on display by Scott—backs into a closet with her space suit, and with the camera angled from below to aim directly at her crotch, we get the close-up of her mons as she slowly raises and opens one leg to give the audience the full view. Ripley is captured in the male gaze in a way that might remind us of an offensive "grabbing" remark made once by Donald Trump. Scott makes sure of it.

She dresses in the suit, buckles in with that speargun phallus thing in hand, and when the monster comes, she opens the hatch, whereupon the monster is sucked out the door. The alien catches itself in the doorway, holding on with tremendous strength.

This is the Not Dead Yet film trope, when the villain or monster comes back one last time to make the audience need a change of underwear before they leave the theater. Ripley has to do something phallic here or die. She aims the speargun at the monster and shoots it in the belly, knocking it out the door, tethered outside now where she can slam the door shut and roast the monster in rocket fuel.[16]

Ellen Ripley is not a woman-identified woman. In fact, she shares a mutual hostility with the only other female crew member. But more than that, in my own associations with feminist scholars and activists, one word that is off the table is "bitch." Yet Ripley, in her frustration with Mother's refusal to stop the activated auto-destruction sequence that Ripley herself initiated, screams at the ship, "You bitch!"[17]

16. Jones is a cat with every one of those nine lives. For some reason, Jones's crate does not get sucked out into space, and when the again semi-nude Ripley gets ready for the trip home, the monster finally vanquished, Jones gets his own Snow White cell to be put into hypersleep for the long trip home.

17. Bearing in mind that Ripley was originally written as a male character, Freud/Lacan return when she nukes Mother, and in destroying mother comes into her (er, his) own. Ripley as gender-decoy conceals this matricidal twist.

This phatic expression is in Ripley's mouth again more than once in the sequels.[18] As Kelsey Lueptow notes, the very commonly and casually used word *bitch*, apart from an actual reference to a female canine, has "hibernating connotations that can perpetuate harmful gender stereotypes."[19] Even when it's a woman who uses it. A gendered term like *bitch* resonates with a whole cluster of patriarchal ideas about women-in-general. Some men casually refer to any and all women as bitches. And when used by women, it calls up that old social trope of women seeing the "other woman" as competition (for the approval, attention, or affection of men). The term used proudly by women as a kind of alternative identity? That's emancipation? Because it means being bad-tempered and uncharitable (to others) and proud of it.[20] Does this "identity" come at the expense, moreover, of other women, who are already scaled between (compliant) good-girl and *bitch*?

The term "plays up sexist stereotypes like menstrual maniacs, hyper-emotional incompetence, and female cattiness incurred by cultural messages that bombard media representations of women."[21] *Bitch* is specifically used for women, which ought to be problematic enough, but when it is applied to men, it is an insult that is saying, "You are like a woman," and that is a very bad thing, something to fight about. Again, woman (*bitch*) is offensive, altogether negative. Any way you look at it, *bitch* is a lose-lose situation for women, sexist to its very core.

Portraying it as realistic speech in films is all fine and well. We portray sexists and women who are broken by internalized oppression in films; but when the strong hero-woman uses it, the term is valorized in a decidedly non-woman-identified sense.

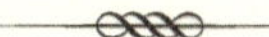

Is Ripley a feminist icon because she kicks ass? We've already seen how Ridley Scott locked onto her genitals with the fetishizing male gaze. Is Ripley a woman emancipated or is she an honorary male/Hot Chick with a Gun?

18. The sequels were unplanned, but when *Alien* cashed out the way it did, Hollywood milked it.

19. Lueptow, "Is 'Bitch' an Example of Internalized Sexism?"

20. Kind of an honorary male thing here, too, because many men have come to take pride in being bad-tempered and uncharitable.

21. Lueptow, "Is 'Bitch' an Example of Internalized Sexism?"

Here is the surprise ending to this chapter. Ripley was originally written as a male. All Scott did was give the part to a female actor. "We really just had the secretary change 'he' to 'she,'" said Producer David Giler.[22]

If this is feminism, if this is emancipation for women, then it simply means women becoming *like* men. And men? We need not change at all. We are still the norm, "and we are no one's bitch."

22. Gallardo and Smith, *Alien Woman*, 16. Imagine now how "You bitch!" sounds coming from the original male character.

3

Clarice Has Three Daddies: Clarice Starling

Silence of the Lambs (1991), a film written by Thomas Harris as both novel and screenplay, and directed by Jonathan Demme, is going to take us back through the same psychosexual territory in some respects that we encountered in *Alien*. Freud and Lacan, to be precise. Before we start, I need to clarify my own position on both Freud and Lacan, both extremely influential European psychoanalysts, Lacan being a kind of theoretical Freudian stepchild.

I am neither a Freudian nor a Lacanian, and for the most part I find them both—in spite of some useful and quite important insights—to be dismissive of women and obsessed with their own male anatomies. But I am not doing a Freudian-Lacanian analysis of either *Alien* or *Silence of the Lambs* because I have a special affinity for this interpretive framework; I am doing "Freudian-Lacanian analysis" of these films because this interpretive framework is self-consciously *already in the films themselves*. We have to enter that framework to understand the inherent logic of the stories. Whether I like their phallus-this-phallus-that[1] way of interpreting the psy-

1. I know, "Lacan is speaking of a *linguistic* phallus" (so sayeth every Lacanian)—which seems even more like bullshit than Freud's fleshier one. And Lacan himself belies this when he himself writes, "One might say that this signifier is chosen as what *sticks out* as most easily seized upon in the *real* of sexual copulation, and also as the most symbolic in the literal (typographical) sense of the term, since it is the equivalent in that relation of the (logical) copula. One might also say that by virtue of its turgidity, it is the image of the vital flow as it is transmitted in generation" (Lacan, *Signification of the Phallus*, 82). Got that? Not a penis. *Sheesh! Of course it's a penis!* Sticks out? Turgid? Flow transmitted in generation? If phallus means the disciplinary function of symbolic thought, then why does it have to be called a pecker and associated with the Father's authority *against* the Mother?

chodynamics of human beings or not, this way of "knowing" is and has been culturally influential for a very long time.

We already think that way, in many respects, because we have assimilated many of these assumptions, preoccupations, and myths—which is what most of their ideas are—reworked myths. *Male gendered* myths from the *Western* canon. This assimilation—as we said in the last chapter—makes patriarchal psychoanalysis a self-fulfilling theory.[2] Euro-bourgeois-man forms phallus-obsessed psychoanalysis; phallus-obsessed psychanalysis forms man (and defines woman as *for*-man).

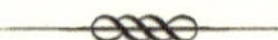

In *Alien*, we had a male character that was switched at the last moment to female by simply changing the pronouns in the screenplay, and we had the *sexual confusion* portrayed visually in the monster her-him-self—in the fanged vagina. In *Silence of the Lambs*, we have *sexual confusion* represented by a female character trying to become an honorary male, pitted against a (monstrous) male character who has a particularly ghastly way of trying to turn himself into a woman. This mirroring is the very superstructure of the unfolding plot.

Clarice Starling, played by Jodie Foster, is a woman student at the FBI Academy, recruited by psychological profiling honcho Jack Crawford, to approach the (now iconic) genius-gastronome-aesthete-serial-killer Hannibal Lecter, in order to identify and capture another serial killer nicknamed "Buffalo Bill"—who exclusively targets "size 14" women.

As we get to know "Bill," we learn that he hates his male identity, and that after being refused transsexual surgery, he takes matters into his own hands by killing and skinning size 14 women, sewing their pelts together to make a "girl-suit" that he can don (changing himself into a "woman") while he capers around, surrounded by moths, in his grisly basement, to the sound of "Goodbye Horses" (Q Lazarus), and accompanied by his yappy toy poodle. In case we don't get it yet and need to be hit over the head, "Bill" tucks his male gonads behind his closed thighs, and admires his "female" pseudo-mons in the mirror.

2. Moi, "From Femininity to Finitude." I'm not attacking psychoanalysis. As Toril Moi points out, "Psychoanalysis has given us a whole series of concepts that are invaluable to feminists and other cultural critics: the unconscious, desire, fantasy, identification, projection, transference, countertransference, alienation, narcissism—the list could continue for a long time."

Clarice, for her part, is constantly set apart from men in the shots of the FBI Academy and elsewhere, seeking in every case to be as asexual as possible, even as she is subjected to the male gaze by other academy students again and again. A male fellow student turns to look at her behind as she runs. An elevator full of males overshadows her tiny, lone, female figure in an elevator. The insipid director of the psychiatric facility holding Lecter leers at her as he suggests she go on a hook-up date with him while she is visiting Baltimore. A psychiatric inmate masturbates as Clarice passes by and slings his semen into her hair as she passes. Lecter, played by Anthony Hopkins, himself constantly fixes her in a kind of hyper-voyeuristic gaze. The male policemen in West Virginia, who are on hand for a victim's autopsy, are shown as a circle of staring eyes. The male gaze is almost a named character in *Silence*.

If the male gaze weren't apparent enough from these scenes, when we first meet "Bill," he is lurking outside a parking lot, lying in wait for his next victim, with a pair of night vision goggles, through which we, the audience, can also project the appropriating gaze in green, night-vision monochrome. Capturing her with his eyes is preamble to her physical capture. Lecter, to Clarice, explaining covetousness: "Don't you feel eyes moving over your body, Clarice?" This, during that crucial interview when he manages to give her an erotic stroke of the finger. As we reach the climax of the film, Clarice herself is caught in the dark in "Bill's" home, as "Bill" tracks her with the male-gaze-goggles and his phallic pistol.

With these highlights, which most readers know by heart from this iconic and immensely popular film, we can orient ourselves on the psychoanalytic subtexts, and on the way sexual confusion is deployed by Harris and Demme to gain and maintain the dramatic tension. Within this psychoanalytic framework, we can see fairly well into the character of Clarice.

Silence of the Lambs began as a novel by Thomas Harris. In terms of its basic plot convention, the book and film are "slashers," horror stories in which women are serially and terrifyingly murdered by a relentless and monstrous killer. One of the tropes in the slasher film genre is the Final Girl.[3] One by one, the (often skimpily clad and/or promiscuous) female characters are bumped off, leaving the lone surviving "final girl," who is less sexualized and more conservatively dressed, often even bookish.[4] In

3. Clover, "Her Body, Himself." Carol Clover coined the phrase "Final Girl" to describe this film trope in 1992.

4. Clover, *Men, Women, and Chain Saws*, 42. "As slasher director Dario Argento puts

Halloween, that was Laurie (played by Jamie Lee Curtis); in *Texas Chain Saw Massacre*, it was Sally (played by Marilyn Burns); in *Nightmare on Elm Street*, the Final Girl was Heather (played by Nancy Thompson). The Final Girl is the one who finally defeats the monster. In *Silence of the Lambs*—which does depart in several ways from typical slasher fare, but without leaving the genre—Clarice Starling is technically, though not thematically, rescued from being the Final Girl by *her* rescue of . . . Damsel in Distress:[5] Catherine Martin, played convincingly by Brooke Smith.

The departures from the Final Girl trope in this film are important, even if they don't fundamentally subvert the trope, because they make *Silence of the Lambs* a more sophisticated piece of filmmaking than most slashers, and because they set up the story to plunge deeper into that atmosphere of Lacanesque sexual confusion that defines Clarice as the reverse image of her adversary, Buffalo Bill, played very creepily by Ted Levine.

The victims in *Silence* are not directly sexualized by the male gaze of the director (the shot of Catherine through the goggles is fairly asexual, though in the book she has just had sex with her boyfriend). These women are not set up (in the film, at least) to pay the wages of (sexual) sin with ghastly deaths. We discover them through grisly crime scene photos on Jack Crawford's office wall, then through an autopsy, and only late in the film when semi-nude photos of the first victim are found hidden in her bedroom.

Clarice herself is pursuing an asexual identity for a socially conservative purpose.[6] Clarice is certainly vulnerable to sexualization and the male gaze, as is emphasized in scene after scene in the film; but her *resistance* to

it, 'I like women, especially beautiful ones. If they have a good face and figure, I would much prefer to watch them being murdered than an ugly girl or a man.' Brian De Palma elaborates: 'Women in peril work better in the suspense genre. It all goes back to the *Perils of Pauline* . . . If you have a haunted house and you have a woman walking around with a candelabrum, you fear more for her than you would for a husky man.' Or Hitchcock, during the filming of The Birds: 'I always believe in following the advice of the playwright Sardou. He said "Torture the women!" The trouble today is that we don't torture women enough.' What the directors do not say, but show, is that 'Pauline' is at her very most effective in a state of undress, borne down upon by a blatantly phallic murderer, even gurgling orgasmically as she dies."

5. The rescuer in this trope being typically male, a role into which Clarice wants to live.

6. Clarice is not aiming to become counter-cultural; she is aiming to become a member of the nation's most powerful law enforcement agency that, apart from the gender subtexts, reflects an essentially conservative worldview.

that sexualization *is the point of view of the director and audience.* This is different from most slasher films that sadistically *eroticize* victimization.

Clarice *overcomes* her own vulnerabilities by *becoming* an honorary male. This "reversal" is what allowed many people to see a feminist thread running through the narrative. I will challenge that, even as it makes a certain sense, in part by pointing out (a book spoiler here) that Harris himself, in the final Starling-Lecter encounter with the novel *Hannibal*, has Clarice become Lecter's lover and new killer companion who will dine with him on the "free-range rude." This final book scene in which she reaches feminine adulthood by being *for-the-phallus* was dramatically altered for the film version to conceal this disturbingly anti-feminist development in the written series from the film audience.

This is not that surprising, however, when one begins to tug at the threads of sexual confusion in *Silence* with Lacanian tweezers. No less a Lacan acolyte than Slovenian philosopher Slavoj Žižek has claimed that Lecter himself *is* a Lacanian, and that *Silence of the Lambs* is really a dramatization of Lecter's psychoanalytical intervention with Clarice,[7] Lecter helping her work out her own symbolic impasse with regard to her recurring fantasy about saving the lamb, so that she can move on and become identified (as she finally does) with the Father/Phallus/symbolic authority. Hey, Lecter is, after all, a European psychiatrist.

With regard to The Father, note that Clarice's character loses her mother before she has an organized memory of her. "My father was everything to me." Raised by her father, she then takes on two more father figures/mentors during the film, Jack Crawford and Hannibal Lecter. What do they help her to do? Catch the monster, who is monstrous because he is a man trying to become a woman . . . by disguising himself in skinned women.

In a mirror image, Clarice is a woman trying to make it in a man's world . . . which she accomplishes by becoming like-a-man, a combination of her three alternative-father figures, her Dad the All-American policeman (her first model), and the antagonists, Crawford (teaching her their trade) and Lecter (giving her self-knowledge and therefore insight). How does she accomplish her transformation? Ultimately, with a gun (penis) that destroys her antagonist/mirror who is gazing at her through the night goggles, getting ready to shoot her with his gun (penis).

7. Žižek, *Looking Awry*, 59.

The Last Girl meets *High Noon*—Gary Cooper with a modestly ignored vagina. And lest we forget, Clarice, the honorary male, is rescuing the female victim, Catherine Martin, trapped in the basement. Substitute a male for Clarice, and you have a classic Damsel in Distress/Slasher trope. Clarice advances as an honorary male, and redeems the world by killing—redemptive violence, once again and too often, being the standard male trope in suspense/action films.

In the same year, another blockbuster film, hailed by some as feminist, featured women coming into their own with guns—*Thelma and Louise*, written by Callie Khouri (who also wrote *Mad Money*, another story of women coming into their own through armed robbery) and directed by none other than Ridley Scott. In this case, the liberated women characters "found themselves" by using guns, then fulfilled themselves through suicide.

Silence of the Lambs' basic storyline, fascinating as it is for all audiences, is still male, still a slasher, still about the serial slaughter of women. If that isn't enough to put the film's feminist *bona fides* into question, then the final novel should. Add to that the Lecter novel before *Silence—Red Dragon*—where we find the crazed killer is made into what he is by an evil, castrating grandmother. Phillip Ellis notes that Harris's female characters tend to be "either victims or villains."[8] Clarice escapes this fate, at least when *Silence* was written and produced, by becoming an honorary male (refusing to be a *victim*, though in the final novel, she becomes Lecter's victim then Nietzschean co-*villain*).

The honorary male is a female character who succeeds in the context of the story by becoming more like men, as men are according to the gender norms of the day, without fundamentally questioning those power structures within which gender—as a social structure that divides power between men and women—is nested. In other words, nothing else changes except that a woman does what only men had done before. Bear in mind that Clarice's sexual-confusion "mirror,"[9] "Buffalo Bill," is fully

8. Ellis, "Before Her Lambs Were Silent," 170.

9. The "mirror stage" is a protean concept that recurs in Lacan, in which one's own identity depends upon actual mirrors or other people as virtual mirrors to validate it. The "primordial" identification is with Mother/The Real, of course, which is tamed, so to speak, through eventual maturity, i.e., identification with the Father/Symbolic Realm/Law.

revealed in his own "monstrosity" during that genital-tuck scene wherein he dresses up as an ethereal woman (an honorary woman). To become an honorary male is to succeed (and identify with the Law). To become an honorary woman is monstrous.

In Lacanian terms, maturity is achieved through identification with the phallus/father/symbolic order. In *Silence of the Lambs*, Clarice's development skips the psychoanalytically purported "problem" of having a mother. Her mother dies when Clarice is young, and Clarice is raised by her father—a law-enforcement officer. Her next father figure is Jack Crawford, who is schooling her in the finer points of law enforcement.[10] Clarice gets a Lacanian leg up, so to speak, by jumping over that "primordial real" of early identification with the Mother, which stands her in good stead—even under the constant and diminishing male gaze of fellow students at the FBI Academy, where she is an asexual "good student." Her final father figure, the one who is also the *psychoanalyst* who brings her to the full identification with the Father, is Lecter.

And Lecter's preparation, then, to commit murder in the final scene is welcomed by the audience. We have come to identify with Lecter and celebrate his violence—because his victims are rude, dislikeable, or whatever—making Lecter himself a male engaged in the business, albeit *beyond the law*, of aesthetically redeeming the world by ridding it of unpleasant but savory people.[11]

10. Lacan, *Écrits*, 67. "It is in the *name of the Father* that we must recognize the support of the symbolic function which, from the dawn of history, has identified his person with the figure of the law."

11. Jennings, *Outlaw Justice*, 114–17. Jennings, in writing about the Apostle Paul's references to "law," falls back on a Lacanian interpretation of law, which is very interesting with regard to Lecter as Clarice's third father and (in the last book) lover and co-conspirator. Lacan, as an intellectual from a very Catholic nation, was deeply interested in St. Paul. In Romans 7:8–11, we encounter the strange language (interpreted by Jennings), "Apart from the law, sin lies dead. I was once apart from [before] the law, but when the commandment came, sin revived and I died. The commandment that was [supposed to be] life became death. For sin finding opportunity in the commandment deceived me and by it killed me."

What are we to make of this? Here is Jennings again: "This becomes, in Lacanian psychoanalytic language, the tale of everyone, who begins life before the Law but then encounters the Law as the symbolic order, as the Law of the father, as the interdiction of desire . . . Instead of restraining what is prohibited, the Law only makes it more attractive or compelling. We thus have a dialectic of Law (as prohibition): the incitement of desire and thence transgression of the Law." This dialectic is apparent between Lecter and Clarice, but also between Lecter and Clarice's predecessor and Lecter's captor, Will Graham—who experiences the *desires* of various psychopaths, as a kind of special gift,

"Bill," on the other hand, has had his development disrupted. "In one of Clarice's meetings with Dr. Lecter," writes Meghan Evans, "Lecter explains that as a child Bill was sexually abused by a male figure (whether it is the father is not known), which explains why Bill covets the female form. [Female] is the gender that has not harmed him, and therefore, one that he would rather embrace . . . Lecter also says in the same scene that Bill 'hates his own identity . . . and he thinks that makes him a transsexual. But his pathology is a thousand times more savage.'"[12]

In the final scene of *Silence of the Lambs*, Clarice is graduating from the FBI Academy, dressed in a suit, whereupon Crawford shakes her hand (a man-to-man gesture of recognition, signaling to the audience that Clarice has achieved equality), and tells her that *her father would be proud.* Surrogate institutional father speaks for biological father, whereupon Clarice gets a phone call from her psychiatric father, Lecter, who congratulates her then heads off to make a meal of the boorish Dr. Chilton.[13]

Lacan applauds. So does liberal feminism. Clarice is now a killer, an enforcer of the law, successfully integrated into the otherwise status quo

---

in order to catch them.

"The dialectical relationship between desire and the Law," writes Lacan, "causes our desire to flare up only in relation to the Law, through which it becomes the desire for death. It is only because of the Law that sin . . . takes on an excessive, hyperbolic character . . . we are in fact led to the point where we accept the formula that without a transgression there is no access to *jouissance* [ecstasy, superabundant vitality, orgasmic pleasure], and to return to St. Paul, that is precisely the function of the Law. Transgression in the direction of *jouissance* only takes place if it is supported by the oppositional principle, by the forms of the Law" (Lacan, *The Ethics of Psychoanalysis*, 83–84).

Of course, in Paul, selfless love—*agape*—offers a way out of this tug-of-war.

12. Evans, "Silence of the Sexes." "When Bill imprisons his newest victim, Catherine Martin, in the well of his basement, and orders her to 'rub the lotion on its skin,' he begins to see Catherine as a human being rather than merely as skin for his suit. As she cries, 'I want to see my mommy,' Bill's lip begins to quiver and his eyes tear up. Then, irritated by the guilt he feels, Bill screams at Catherine and mockingly mimics her panic when she sees the fingernail of his last victim stuck in the wall of the well. His guilt here transforms into a perverted pleasure at reminding himself that he has power over the frightened Catherine. In a similar fashion, his stereotypical feminine behavior, his quivering lip and tears, transforms into stereotypical masculine behavior, as he demonstrates his power. This depiction of Bill demonstrates that his goal to achieve femininity threatens real women, not only his female victims, but also Clarice who is trying to slough off her own female identity."

13. The *He Had it Coming* trope, in which—even though illegal or even immoral—a fatal event is attenuated by the audience's cultivated dislike of the character, so the death doesn't distract us from the flow of the story.

Establishment. Little do we know, in Harris's most pseudo-Nietzschean flourish, Clarice will leave that status quo, one book later (film sanitation notwithstanding), to join Lecter as a re-feminized, sexually appealing lover, after eating her own future nemesis, another FBI agent. Therapy complete, she is now herself beyond the Law, existing finally *for* the phallus.

4

Earning a Penis to Kill Arabs: Jordan O'Neil

Oh Ridley, Ridley, we keep bumping into you, brother!

It is 1997 now, and Ridley Scott is releasing another one: *GI Jane.* My penance for many sins was sitting through this film, as will be yours when you watch it. Nonetheless, it deserves a place of honor in this book for its exemplification of the honorary male/masculinity-constructed-as-violence-and-conquest trope.

We won't dwell overmuch on the silly plot contrivances, or incredibly predictably bad writing, or the nonexistent basic research (Army and Marine units undergoing BUD training in the Navy? US Navy SEAL training as the most rigorous training in history? Helicopters in every scene no matter what? Trainers firing single shots into infiltration courses from sniper rifles? Explosive Ordnance Disposal as Special Operations? Wrong, wrong, wrong, wrong, wrong). That aside, however, we will concentrate here on the tropes, the gender narratives, and the ideological backdrop of *G.I. Jane.*

I'm going to pick a strange place to start, though: the Stabbed-in-the-Back myth, a political trope perfected by Hitler and his minions, and one redeployed by right-wingers in the United States to account for the US defeat in Vietnam, that world-historic affront to American national masculinity. It goes like this: brave and virtuous soldiers fight for a long time, gaining ground against the despised enemy, but weak-willed and opportunistic politicians "stab them in the back," by seeking peace . . . er, surrendering . . . which is the same thing. Definitely not Real Man stuff.

The Nazi Party played this like a tenor saxophone over Germany's defeat in World War I; and disgruntled old white men with POW-MIA stickers on their vehicles in the US are still saying the same thing about Vietnam—a theme that got major play in another iconic and outrageously bad film, *First Blood*, with its now archetypical kill-kill protagonist, Rambo.[1] Fewer now, because we are dying off, but still . . . this is an outline of the ideological backdrop for *G.I. Jane*—that contrast between the virtuous warrior and the sly, self-serving politician.

Not surprisingly, the sly politician in *G.I. Jane* is the only other major "feminist" character in the film: Senator Lillian DeHaven, played by Anne Bancroft. It is interesting that between the two female characters in *G.I. Jane*, one is an opportunistic "feminist," and the other disavows feminism altogether, motivated purely by the desire for advancement (like Clarice Starling) and patriotism (like Starling). The character Jordan O'Neil[2] (played by Demi Moore) explicitly states that she is in training as a career opportunity and not as part of any social movement. It is equally interesting that the two main female characters will eventually be paired off against one another. A standard for filmmakers' fave form of dramatic-tension-producing "female misogyny" is the Backstabbing Bitch trope, closely related to the Stabbed in the Back myth in the way it feminizes treachery. Jordan O'Neil will, in the end, of course, identify with the boys.

She will do more than identify, though. She will shear off her hair. She will quit menstruating. And in a climactic scene, where she beats her main male antagonist in a fist fight, she trumpets over his fallen body, in her best frat-boy fashion, "Suck my dick!" She not only lays claim to a phallus for herself, she engages in that timeworn pattern of probative masculinity, the demand for sexual tribute as a trophy from a beaten foe. And it is with this frankly weird line in the film, that she is suddenly and almost magically accepted by the rest of the guys.

Once Jane earns her penis by beating the snot out of her sadistic instructor, the other fellas suddenly accept her. "Suck my dick! Yuk-yuk," and she is in the club. She can show violent aggression and conflate (penile) sex with hostile domination. She's a boy, at last!

But wait! As in any coming-of-age male military fantasy, what's the good of that training to become a lethal weapon if you can't use it? Never fear. In Act 3, Jane goes to war. In another plot device that would never happen in the actual world of the actual US military, her training unit (training units are not combat units, folks; they are not even organized for it) is on an exercise, when an American unit gets stranded and surrounded by . . . Bad

1. RAM-bo(ne). Beleaguered masculinity at its aggressive phallic best.

2. Not really named "G.I. Jane," but the play on "G.I. Joe" marks this as an honorary male trope from the outset.

Arabs.[3] No other unit in the entire United States Armed Forces is available to rescue our stranded heroes—presumably because the whole rest of the massive American military apparatus is tied up fighting Bad Arabs elsewhere—so Jane gets to join her comrades in Real Combat, where she can become a Real (wo)Man by killing Bad Arabs. Ah, equality!

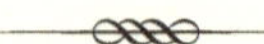

I'm going to continue raining on the parade here with another gap between reality and film about the military that isn't just about bad research and filmmakers' affinity for jazzing up the set in almost every scene with hovering helicopters, colored smoke, and fireballs.

The actual military is an institution that is at its very core misogynistic. The enterprise of war is at its core misogynistic. These things—and here is where I will step on the toes of liberal feminist fantasies as well as garden-variety patriotism—cannot be changed, because of the peculiar historical relationship between conquest-masculinity and war. War reproduces conquest-masculinity; and conquest-masculinity reproduces war. In ideology (and film), this dynamic is supported by women's inclusion *only* as honorary males. In reality, military institutions are horrifically hostile places for women, and this has not been substantially changed by the inclusion of more women.

If any woman wants to vastly multiply her opportunities for hostile objectification, sexual harassment, sexual assault, and rape, the United States Armed Forces is the right place to go. It has the best rape demographic—lots of men between eighteen and thirty years old. It has the right ingredients for a super-rape culture—young men indoctrinated into violence, associating with other men like them, misogynistic to the core, combined with long hours where women are left with these men day and night. And best of all, it is a self-protective bureaucracy that will scapegoat a few vulnerable enlisted men for off-color remarks to prove their anti-harassment *bona fides* to the public, while engaging in massive cover-ups of systematic rape and abuse, especially if officers or senior NCOs are the perpetrators. Military ethics are purely instrumental.

The other thing these pro-military films never depict is the moral hazard of war itself. People are allowed to do things in war with a certain

3. Bad Arab(s) is the racist convention that is accepted in Hollywood right now, since they've been forced by cultural pressure to scale back on Bad Negroes, Bad Japs, Bad Indians, and so on.

impunity that they could not do otherwise. Vehicular hit and run (of anyone who failed to get out of the way) was a very common example in Iraq. Once the people who failed to accept a foreign invasion and occupation started building command-detonated mechanical ambushes (improvised explosive devices), commanders told their vehicle drivers to drive at warp speed and ignore slow-down obstacles like bicycles, dogs, and pedestrians. Since Iraqis had no legal recourse nor even any way of knowing which vehicles with which drivers from which base had just run over their child, there were no consequences. I have personally spoken with several former soldiers who have this particular beautiful memory to carry around with them for the remainder of their lives. There are plenty of other things, of course, like shooting a carful of people who fail to follow commands shouted in English, or that loony bastard in your unit that shoots anyone with a shovel and claims the victim was burying an IED. Or the bystander victims that get hit by stray rounds and bombs. Or the stories of the grunts who engage in thrill-killing while on patrol. If you're really the thoughtful type, you might even begin to wonder what gave you the right to be here in someone else's country pushing them around in the first place.

The usual narrative is that the military has its bad "exceptions," and that soldiers become damaged by the bad things they see. If there are bad exceptions, someone needs to explain how the bad exceptions all end up in the same units—because this stuff is done by units, not individuals. And, as I said in *Borderline*, "My experience of war is that war, as a practice, does not inculcate honor as often as hatred, hostility, cruelty, and the fragmentation of the soldier's personality. Bad soldiers do not make war a bad thing. War invariably makes soldiers do bad things, and we become what we do."[4]

Anuradha Kristina Bhagwati, a former Marine officer, in conversation with Setsu Shigematsu, a feminist scholar-activist, told Shigematsu:

> A large part of me was drawn to these superwomen icons, and shaped my desire to fight the man in whatever institution I was in. If it weren't for Demi Moore playing the role of *GI Jane*, I might never have joined the military. One of the horrible results of the Hollywood version of the sexy woman killer is that the causes and effects of violence are very rarely explored. Killing is basically a livelihood for these fantasy women. They rarely have to deal with the warping of their soul or psyche.[5]

To which Shigematsu replied:

4. Goff, *Borderline*, 102.
5. Shigematsu and Bhagwati, "Women of Color Veterans," 100–101.

> These popular representations of women's empowerment through their ability to compete with and outdo men through acts of physical prowess and militarized violence have become one of the ways in which representations of token and fantasy women not only misrepresent women's experiences in the military, but operate to normalize the mass industrial violence and obscure the gravity of our socioeconomic crises that the cycle of warfare will only exacerbate . . . Many feminists who identify themselves as anti-military and anti-war may not pay heed to how the militarization of women may in fact constitute a deep crisis for US feminism.[6]

One cannot fully understand militarism without an account of violent masculinity, and one cannot fully understand violent masculinity without an account of militarism. They are kind of a cultural yin-yang, each embracing and reproducing the other. This is one reason that the failure to address militarism in the context of an allegedly feminist narrative is even more problematic than the failure to address race, class, and nationality. Not because generic women can't do what generic men do in the military—as former career military, I can promise you that there are some women who can absolutely perform any task performed by men in the execution of their responsibilities as soldiers. But militarism, the nationalistic elevation of the status of military action and war as the nation's highest form of "sacrificial service," has its roots in a practice and ideology that historically associates masculinity (even with a few women now added) with the idea that *violence is virtuous*—the selfsame masculinity that devalues, exploits, and dominates women. The corresponding reality is that, as a special form of masculine virtue, the willingness to kill perfect strangers requires a form of psychological compartmentalization, suppression of *misericordia*[7] or empathy, and the amplification of those traits already gendered male—cold instrumentality, aggression, and cruelty. This amplification of traits that are gendered male, apart from the moral issues involved, when considered virtuous, in turn devalue those traits that are its opposite and historically gendered female. This is what underwrites the long-standing and still persistent culture of misogyny that characterizes military organizations.

When Andrea Dworkin said that "equality" means becoming the murderer instead of the murdered, this is precisely what she meant. This is

6. Ibid., 101.

7. A term I prefer to the more psychological term, "empathy," from the Latin for "a merciful heart," because of its Christian meaning—that mysterious bridge of mercy extending between God's love and human misery.

not sex-gender emancipation. It is American exceptionalism—the idea that the United States, as the Great Nation responsible to both police the world and transform it in its own image, has the unique right to intervene in the affairs of foreign nations—that is the very ideological canvas upon which these war stories are painted.

In films like *G.I. Jane*, the scenarios are set up in such a way that the Good Guys (and honorary male Good Gynes) kill only wicked armed combatants. In real war, non-combatant deaths outnumber combatant deaths by more than three to one. Depending on where the war is, the percentage of those noncombatant deaths who are women and children can range from twenty-five percent, for example in Iraq, where soldiers killed noncombatant "military-aged" males more frequently based on suspicion of their combatant status, to half female where bombing has been the primary method of attack. This does not take into account loss of public services to pregnant women and women with children, skyrocketing incidences of rape, untreated disease from contaminated water and malnutrition, maternal death, and suicide.[8] One might ask the *G.I. Jane* "feminist" the same question put to her colleagues by former slave Sojourner Truth in 1827: "Ain't I a woman?" Aren't the women on the receiving end of US wars women?

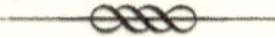

Traditionally, the role of women in war films has been associated with "just war"[9] rationalizations. Just war, or *jus ad bellum*, is only just if war is practiced in response to a *casus belli*, or cause for belligerence. Most people see self-defense, once attacked, as *casus belli*, for example, and many believe coming to the aid of an ally or the helpless when they are attacked is *casus belli*.[10] In war and other violent practices (e.g., lynching), the "protection of women and children," or the "protection of womanhood," or the "protection of white womanhood," etc., has provided the *casus belli*. Filmmakers love this one; and women (who are the equals of children in their helplessness) become what Béatrice Châteauvert-Gagnon calls "Beautiful Souls" requiring "Just Warriors" to protect them.[11]

8. Ormhaug, "Armed Conflict Deaths."

9. As in *justice*, not "just" as in "merely" or "only."

10. The other criterion for "just" war is *ultima ratio*, meaning only as a last resort, but this one has been erased by preemptive war doctrines.

11. Châteauvert-Gagnon, "Militarized Femininity," para. 1.

What is particularly interesting about Jordan O'Niel's character is that before she can become the "just warrior," she has to be de-feminized, undergoing a sex change that includes toughening up, becoming amenorrheac, shaving her head, smoking cigars (wink!), laying claim to a figurative weaponized phallus, and finally killing Bad Arabs—interesting because of what this implies about actually embodied females who do not transsexualize into (honorary) men. Un-transitioned bodies remain fixed inside the earlier binary as Beautiful Soul cum *casus belli*, until particular women are singled out for whatever transgression of the binary. That, in turn, places them outside the circle of gender-trust. There is no win here for women. There is either the honorary male or the Beautiful Soul or the Backstabbing Bitch trope exemplified by Senator DeHaven.

Women, as everyday women, are not only not represented and not valorized, they are generalized back into the same sets of patriarchal stereotypes and gender norms that they were subjected to in the first place. The same, white, youth-obsessed, compulsorily heterosexual norms.[12]

12. Rich, "Compulsory Heterosexuality." The total title of Rich's now canonical feminist essay was "Compulsory Heterosexuality and Lesbian Existence." This was not about "lesbian" existence or experience as an erotic choice, even though same-sex erotic experience was one component of her description of "lesbianism." For Rich, compulsory heterosexuality was about the strict expectations of the patriarchal gender binary, within which men identified with men and women identified with men. A lesbian existence, for Rich, is women identifying first with other women—as alike in experience, as cherished sisters, and not as potential competition for the attention and approval of men. Women who are attracted to men, and even in sexual relationships with men, are just as trapped, according to Rich, by a system of "compulsory heterosexuality" as women who are not.

"I have chosen to use the terms *lesbian existence* and *lesbian continuum*," writes Rich, "because the word *lesbianism* has a clinical and limiting ring. *Lesbian existence* suggests both the fact of the historical presence of lesbians and our continuing creation of the meaning of that existence I mean the term *lesbian continuum* to include a range—through each woman's life and throughout history—of woman-identified experience; not simply the fact that a woman has had or consciously desired genital sexual experience with another woman. If we expand it to embrace many more forms of primary intensity between and among women, including the sharing of a rich inner life, the bonding against male tyranny, the giving and receiving of practical and political support."

Compulsory heterosexuality is the cultural-ideological foundation of patriarchal power, dividing men and women into complementary spheres bridged by an axis of domination and subordination. The male machismo portrayed in *GI Jane* is not criticized as an instance of compulsory heterosexuality; it is *reinforced as necessary* in the Protective Role. Carole Pateman describes this as the "sexual contract," wherein the (Beautiful Soul) "weaker" sex exchanges obedience for protection from the "stronger" sex (Just Warrior).

5

Recapturing Normal from the Zombie Apocalypse: Selena

28 Days Later is two overlapping genres: the contagion narrative and zombie apocalypse.[1] Good writing, great direction and acting, excellent film composition and editing, convincing special effects that don't overwhelm the scenes, and well-adapted background music are all combined with a strong story to make this an edge-of-your-seat classic. That's not to say that the film is above criticism, as we will see, but at least it's not Hollywood gruel like *G.I. Jane*. Before we get to the female lead character, Selena, however, we need to look at the film's dual genre to establish some context.

As a long time Haitiphile, I have to start with zombies. The history of the zombie is quite revealing, because it is associated with Haiti, even though zombies are an American invention. As Paul Farmer pointed out in *The Uses of Haiti*,[2] the first independent black nation, one born of a slave rebellion, has been attacked and undermined from its inception by "white" nations that needed a standing example of proof of an inhering black deviance and black incapacity for self-governance—with the policies of France and the US to cripple the nation at every turn to make it appear true. And so Haiti came to be associated in the white mind with some fundamental deviance; and this association prepared the white mind to project its most lurid fears back onto Haiti.

1. Dinello, "Vampires, Viruses, and Zombies." Dinello writes: "Contagion is the dominant horror of the 21st century, an era marked by epidemics of terror, war, and economic crisis. Just as atomic anxiety infused Cold War-era pop culture, fear of contagion dominates recent pop culture in the form of apocalyptic zombie plagues, viral pandemics, infectious vampires, parasitized bodies, and microbe-caused mutations."

2. Farmer, *Uses of Haiti*, 278.

Between 1791 and 1804, when the Haitian rebel armies were beating the pants off of Napoleon's best (a disastrous blow to the myth of white supremacy), Napoleon—who was fighting in Europe, too—started to run out of money. That's why the Louisiana Purchase happened in 1803, adding some or all of Louisiana, Arkansas, Northern Texas, Oklahoma, Missouri, Kansas, Colorado, Iowa, Nebraska, Minnesota, both Dakotas, and Wyoming, as well as a bit of Saskatchewan to the holdings of the United States. France had claimed this indigenous land and sold the claim to the United States to replenish the Little General's war treasury. Bonaparte lost the war in Haiti less than a year later, and things continued to go downhill for him afterwards.

French slave owners in Haiti, with many of their slaves, decamped to New Orleans,[3] and the Haitian slaves—seventy percent having been born in Africa—brought an amalgam of native rituals and beliefs, which were syncretically combined with aspects of French Catholicism. Those beliefs and rituals were further mixed with Native American beliefs and rituals, and this amalgam came to be known as Voudon, or in street speech, voodoo—a popular spirituality. Beliefs and stories about voodoo then circulated among whites, where they were embellished by white people's often paranoid imagination of black cultures. It wasn't until around 1930 that the popular idea of voodoo incorporated zombies—the walking dead. White American culture, especially Hollywood, with drivel like *The Serpent and the Rainbow*, projected its racial fears into the zombie. The rest, as they say, is history.[4]

This individual racial zombie was then replaced by a new kind of zombie, zombies exhibiting herd behavior. In *Night of the Living Dead*, the 1968 camp-cult classic by George Romero, hordes of slow-moving but relentless reanimated corpses roam the streets in pursuit of human flesh to devour—brains preferred. In Romero's film there is brief speculation that the reanimation of corpse herds is being caused by radioactivity from a returning space probe, but this is a minor sop to causal calculation, the main attraction being the advancing horror of smelly, sluggish, brain-eating cadavers. A few people whose kids had been traumatized by the film wanted the courts to declare *Night of the Living Dead* a form of "violence pornography." Given what kids can see nowadays, including the television series *The Walking Dead*, which is a kicked-up version of *Night*

3. Bell, "Haitian Immigration," para. 3–8.

4. Moreman and Rushton, *Race, Oppression, and the Zombie*, 14–15.

of the Living Dead, the campaign to nip the "violence pornography" of the zombie in the bud has apparently failed.

The Walking Dead has herd zombies, but it also employs another theme—the patriarchal survival fantasy, in which the key to survival (redemption) is still the Man with a Gun, even when it involves women and women with guns. Because a bite contaminates you and makes you a zombie, *The Walking Dead* is also a contagion narrative.

This will take a little history, too.

All good fun.

In 2002, Barbara Duden and Silja Samerski introduced a new term: *pop gene*. The *pop gene* is short form for *popular gene*, and it doesn't mean the gene with the most friends. *Pop gene* doesn't refer, except in passing, to actual genetic science either. *Pop gene* is a vague yet potent *impression* of what genes are, the *popular imagination* of genes that has a vague and very inexact notion of actual genetic science. In pop-imagination, the pop-gene is one form of collective magical thinking. The "gene" becomes symbolic, an *idea*, independent of actual genes, an idea with tremendous power.

Samerski and Duden are both also interested in the history of the experience of pregnancy, and how—over time—this experience has been transformed into a "risk management" exercise requiring the mediation of highly specialized experts. The pop-gene has driven this risk-management medicalization paradigm. So what about zombies? Hold tight. We're getting there.

Samerski, a German, traced the use of the term *risk* in her own culture and found that in the early twentieth century, risk was a merchant's term. As cars became ubiquitous, *risk* was associated with the dangers of car traffic.

> But today, sick people, pregnant women and healthy persons, they all live under the shadow of "risk". When I read the science page of my newspaper, when my health shop informs me about food options or when I go for a routine check to my gynecologist—everywhere I am in the danger of absorbing risks. For years, my neighbor lives in anxiety because of her increased risk of breast cancer. She worries incessantly about every medical check up and studiously pores over all the guides on "Breast fitness—How to reduce your risk of breast cancer". Almost none of my friends escaped becoming a risk carrier as soon as they were diagnosed "pregnant" by a gynecologist. I remember very well when one of my friends desperately rang my doorbell after the physician had urged her to choose between two risks: The risk of giving birth to a handicapped child and the risk of an abortion induced by the test.[5]

5. Samerski, "Risk Anxiety and the Myth of Informed Decision Making," 1.

This loss of autonomy to experts, based in some cases on the internalization of the *pop gene*, has transformed many people into obsessive "risk managers." It is relatively new; but it points to the ways that popular misconceptions can be transformed into popular obsessions.

Now, at last, we come back to zombies and contagion.

In the late nineteenth and early twentieth century, Western Europe and the United States were gripped by something called the social hygiene movement. The popular (mis)conception then, which still prevails today, was what we might call the *pop germ*.

Ever since Pasteur's germ theory and the partially successful employment of carbolic acid as a surgical disinfectant during the American Civil War, the discovery of the role of particular microorganisms in medical pathologies has been translated into the popular imagination as *germophobia*. And the way to protect oneself from "germs" is through sterilization. The fact that the overwhelming majority of microorganisms—a classification by size only—are either benign to humans or beneficial has not blunted this fear. In fact, to this day, one can see television ads representing "germs" as disgusting cartoon-monsters, the solution being the liberal application of this or that product to "leave surfaces germ free."

The *social hygiene movement* of the early twentieth century simply extrapolated this phobia from microorganisms to whole societies, with a synergetic boost from social Darwinism, which led to a vigorous American eugenics movement. Affluent white people not only saw "social hygiene" as a public health movement, but poor and racially othered people as the equivalent of "germs." Germs and "genes," the *pop gene* of that era seen in the light of selective breeding, these ideas—including aggressive support for eugenics—were advocated by liberal and conservative alike well into the twentieth century, until the special earnestness of Hitler's eugenic programs was exposed after the war, temporarily slamming on the brakes of open support for eugenics.[6]

Even after Hitler's illumination of the *eugenic* moral hazard, however, the metaphorical power of disease and sociopolitical hygiene retained its force. J. Edgar Hoover frequently referred to communism, for example, as a "virus." Today, the rapid spread of a story over the internet is called "viral."

6. Goff, *Borderline*, 299–311. Eugenics is still routinely practiced, but the eugenic choices have been privatized.

The contagion narrative in film has its symbolic roots in this history, and more generally in the way cultures have understood purity and pollution, as in Mary Douglas's anthropology, to define boundaries for millennia. Priscilla Wald calls the specific form of contagion narrative that became popular in the 1990s and increasingly popular in the past few years, an "outbreak narrative." She relates this popular narrative to the serial discoveries of various communicable diseases, HIV in particular, followed by travelling maladies like SARS and Ebola.

> The outbreak narrative—in its scientific, journalistic, and fictional incarnations—follows a formulaic plot that begins with the identification of an emerging infection, includes discussion of the global networks throughout which it travels, and chronicles the epidemiological work that ends with its containment.[7]

The standard outbreak narrative described by Wald ends with the triumph of science over these threats that have penetrated our boundaries, and sets up the scientific establishment in a kind of guardian role for a world where traditional boundaries begin to seem dangerously permeable. In film, we see this narrative in *And the Band Played On* and other "based-on-the-true-story" accounts.

Outbreak and contagion narratives are always in danger of reinforcing the *medicalization* of society wherein cultural, moral, and even legal norms are giving way to medical descriptions of behaviors considered aberrant, with medical solutions near at hand—which include copious pharmaceuticals and some institutionalizations. ADHD, for example, describes a set of behaviors that were in greater or lesser force apparent in children before they were confined for six hours a day in compulsory schools; but rather than ask if children should be thus confined, we *describe* the reactions of many children to that confinement as *pathological*, and prescribe drugs to inhibit these reactions. Again, this process of *medicalization* surrenders our autonomy, practical and moral, to a collection of experts in the radical monopoly called Medicine.

Contagion narratives draw the line between the healthy and the infected as boldly as older films drew the line between the Good Guys and the implacable threat, and set up a new risk equation where The Threat, now existential, can come up anywhere, at any time.[8]

7. Wald, *Contagious*, 2.

8. Carroll, Jordan, "The Aesthetics or Risk." Carroll explains, "Like victims of manufactured risk, zombies cannot predict the self-destructive outcome of their actions. The zombie outbreak signifies the horror of the unperceived, unanticipated, and often

There is more than one way, medicalization aside, to characterize contagion narratives. Returning to *Night of the Living Dead*, let's compare Wald's contagion narrative and the triumph of science to the zombie story. The irredeemability of the infected/the zombie creates a situation wherein what is called for is not science, but a reassertion of naked violence like the kind that drives *Walking Dead* and *28 Days Later*. In some cases, this contagion narrative serves up male post-apocalyptic, survivalist fantasies. In this regard, contagion/contamination/zombie narratives like *World War Z*, *Resident Evil*, and *Dawn of the Dead* establish the basis for tempo-task mass killing, which allows men (and their Hot Chicks with Guns) to prove their mettle by dealing out death (to the dangerous dead). These can be cross-categorized with other post-apocalyptic genres—post-nuclear and alien invasion, e.g., *Mad Max*, *Independence Day*, and *Cloverfield*.

28 Days Later, even though it departs from other male post-apocalyptic, survivalist fantasies, and even though it is, in its production values, superior to most, and even though it significantly departs from this genre in particular and powerful ways, is exactly that—a male post-apocalyptic, survivalist fantasy. The inclusion of Selena, played to the hilt by Naomie Harris, not a token female at all, and a black woman to boot, as a co-equal lead with white male protagonist, Jim, makes the fundamental masculinity of this narrative far less apparent than it usually is. *28 Days Later* is a film that has an *explicit* anti-christological theme with regard to the uses of violence, and that is resolved in the most conservative sense with regard to redemptive violence and *masculinity*.

Karl Martin wrote a detailed exposition of (pseudo) Christian themes in *28 Days Later*,[9] in which he showed how and how often Director Danny Boyle (*Trainspotters*, *The Beach*, *Slumdog Millionaire*), a former altar boy, ironically employed Christian music, metaphor, and imagery to translate Alex Garland's (*The Beach*, *Ex Machina*) screenplay for *28 Days Later* into this highly popular 2002 Gen X thriller, whose majority audience—and this is important—was young white men under thirty years of age.[10]

The film opens with a restrained, partially tranquilized chimpanzee, surrounded by television monitors displaying newsreel footage of horrific mass

self-reflexive dangers that arise in the contemporary era—what Ulrich Beck names "risk society." Moreover, whereas earlier forms of hazard were personal or at least placeable, the zombie is global and diffuse. Zombies constitute what Eugene Thacker calls 'fleshy networks of infection'—a danger that is noncentralized and massively distributed."

9. Martin, "Failure of a Pseudo-Christian Community."

10. Lee, "28 Days Later," para. 4.

violence. We pan over to the security monitors and see a black-clad team of animal rights activists breaking into the facility to liberate the chimps. We don't know it yet, but within minutes, if we put on our thinking caps, we will realize that this government lab is developing a biowar weapon in the form of a virus, called Rage. Infection transforms the host into a hyperaggressive, highly contagious beater and biter, who strangely enough recognizes others of "the infected," as we come to know them, and does not attack them. In fact, we have the Herd Zombie trope here, for pack monsters internally compelled to attack only those who are uninfected. Think *Walking Dead* or *I Am Legend*. Mary Douglas's thesis about in-groups is dramatically amplified.

Government conspiracies, the basis of the Deep State Paranoia genre, are a popular device for contagion and monster narratives (*Alien*, *Stranger Things*, *Resident Evil*), but in *28 Days Later*, the plague that is presumably created by the government (and, significantly, let loose by *anti*-government activists) *destroys* the known government. Immediately after the activists release the Rage virus on the world, we go to a scene 28 days hence, where our protagonist, Jim (played by Cillian Murphy), lies emaciated in a hospital bed hooked up to dead monitors and dried out IVs. When he escapes the hospital and eventually joins up with two of the uninfected, he demands to know, "What about the government?" Selena informs him there is no government. "There's got to be a government," he insists. "They're in a bunker or a plane."

Civilizational breakdown becomes a key theme in the film, contrasted with what Martin calls the "pseudo-Christian community" of Jim and three of his fellow uninfected survivors.

Selena, then, is the female lead. Young, black, trained as a pharmacist—when we first meet her, she and another survivor named Mark are Jim's rescuers. She leads the three, even in close combat with "the infected," like a military commando. She is smart, decisive, efficiently ruthless, and painfully realistic. She is pretty, without a doubt, but not overtly sexualized in the opening scenes, where she is clad in a trench coat, with a kind of centurion's helmet hairdo, carrying a machete in her hand at all times. In practice and temperament, Selena is a soldier. When Mark is bitten in a confrontation with the infected, she unhesitatingly dispatches him with her machete in a gruesome splatter scene, telling the surviving Jim that if she suspects he's infected, she'll do him "in a heartbeat."

The tempo task is a soldier character's meat and potatoes. The Russian film director Sergei Eisenstein coined the term "tempo task" as part of his critique of D. W. Griffith's filmic paean to the KKK, *The Birth of a Nation*. The tempo task is a set-up in the film's story where time is running out, and for the victim—then generally a white woman Beautiful Soul—to be saved, the rescuers had to set aside the rules as well as their moral scruples to get the job done in time. Ann Kibbey translated the tempo task to the post-9-11 conjuncture, when we used the same rationale to justify torture.

> Liberals . . . have had difficulty in believing that a much-discredited American film genre, the Western, could suddenly be structuring and mandating U.S. political rhetoric. It is—from Bush's "Wanted dead or Alive" Bin Laden poster, to Colin Powell's insistence that "time is running out" as we cut to the chase, to the numerous U.S. television and print media that report daily on the "Showdown" or "Standoff" with Iraq.[11]

The justifications are always hypothetical situations where the bomb is about to go off in the subway. "Would you, oh effeminate snowflake that you are, refuse to torture the evildoer rather than pull out his fingernails to discover where the bomb is and defuse it before it kills thousands?" While such urgently constructed scenarios are nearly non-existent in reality, they are the stuff of many films, including the execrable *Zero Dark Thirty*, directed by Katherine Bigelow, about the US hit of Osama bin Laden. Bigelow introduced just such a last-minute torture scene to discover the whereabouts of bin Laden before he could get away, *even though no such thing happened in conjunction with the actual operation*. It was *gratuitous* pro-torture propaganda.

A zombifying contagion like the Rage virus is an ongoing *tempo task*, a situation where all the old moral scruples have to be set aside. In the beginning of the film, Jim is reluctant to embrace the tempo-task mentality or Selena's keep-up-or-die soldier's commitment to survival. In fact, as Martin notes, Jim begins by exercising a decidedly Christian sensibility—at least from Director Boyle's perspective.

Jim roams the empty streets of London after waking to an empty urban landscape from his hospital bed, and he eventually—as the sun gets low—heads to a church. He mounts the church steps, and we see a massive cross hanging by the wall, and alongside it graffiti that says, "The end is extremely fucking nigh," a mocking paraphrase of the last chiliastic street preachers. Jim continues in, finding the pews stacked with corpses—where others have likewise sought the church for their fruitless refuge. When Jim

11. Kibbey, "Gender and the American Ideology of War," para. 1.

calls out, two of "the infected"—the first he's seen—pop up from the piled dead and begin scuttling toward the stairs. Then the priest himself arrives, infected, hissing, hacking, and red-eyed, convulsing with mindless reptilian aggression toward Jim until, at the last moment, Jim knocks the priest away with a sack of canned soda, muttering to himself as he runs away, "I shouldna done that." Hit a priest, even though . . .

In a latter scene, before Selena has killed Mark, as the three companions head out to find Jim's dead family, the background music is Perry Alleyne singing "Abide with Me," a Christian hymn. It is coming back down that same road, Mark dead now, that Selena delivers her soldier's speech to Jim: kill without hesitation if you want to live. Christian church fails to protect. Christian morals fail to protect. As Karl Martin says,

> The gospel hymn's lyrics follow Jim's actions so closely that it seems as though this might be what is playing in Jim's memory as he finds his parents. Secondly, the lyrics of the gospel hymn stress comfort offered to the individual in the midst of a crisis. The repeated use of the first person is one indication of the private nature of the comfort offered. The temptation sung of in "Abide With Me" seems to be to give up in despair. Perhaps following the pattern of his parents, and much more than the other two survivors, Jim seems tempted in this way. Early in the film, neither Mark nor Selena seems tempted to despair. Rather, they are focused on violent resistance to the infected . . . The Christian message of the hymn may bring comfort to Jim . . . but it provides little guidance in a world swarming with enraged plague victims.[12]

The message of the film is traditionally gendered, even with the early gender subversion of Selena as the warrior and Jim as the nurturing nice guy.

Selena and Jim meet Frank and Hannah, father and daughter, holed up in a fortified high-rise apartment. Selena and Jim enter the apartment under duress, "the infected" hot on their heels in the dark, dingy stairwells, but once inside, they encounter Christmas lights and Christmas music playing. Frank—appearing as a formidable black armored behemoth—removes his makeshift armor and emerges as a smiling, soft-spoken, middle-aged man who asks teenage daughter Hanna to find the *crème de menthe* for a toast to their guests.

They settle in, and when Jim and Selena are talking, she castigates Jim for calling Frank and Hannah "nice people," telling him that his concern ought

12. Martin, "Failure of a Pseudo-Christian Community."

to be whether they'll slow him down. This disagreement about who would or would not leave people behind highlights again the contrast between Selena's soldier/survival ethic and Jim's basic (Christian) altruism.

Over time, however, after the four companions go in search of "salvation," as advertised on a repeating radio broadcast, and after a kind of faux-family shopping spree and another confrontation with "the infected," they take off through the countryside to the background of "Ave Maria" (that's right) and end up camping at an old church ruin (yes), where they see four healthy horses (two adults and two juveniles) cavorting in a field, a reflection of how they themselves are becoming a family. With the "In Paradisium" of Fauré's *Requiem* in the background, this is when Selena has a change of heart, as she grows increasingly close to Hannah. In this pivotal scene, she admits to Jim that she was wrong in earlier saying "surviving is as good as it gets." She has learned to love, and she even pecks Jim on the cheek. Frank has become the father (Jim even calls him "Dad," when Frank shakes him to stop a nightmare), Selena and Jim the older brother and sister, and Hannah the younger sister. Selena, the soldier who eschewed any form of family, is now embracing it again, moving her back into the "correct" gender column. This is what Martin calls the formation of a pseudo-Christian community in the film.[13]

Off they head, the family of four, to the intersection described by the soldiers in the radio broadcast, promising, "*Salvation* is here. The answer to infection is here" (italics added). And so our family seeks salvation no longer from pseudo-Christ, *but from soldiers*. While this is certainly a common refrain in film—officially sanctioned violent men with guns standing watch on the frontier between civilization and chaos—*28 Days Later* flips this tired script and makes the soldiers they encounter more dangerous than the zombies. Frying pan. Fire.

This is where the film appears to become really transgressive even as it slips into a deeply conservative convention, perhaps reflecting the moral confusion experienced by the writer's generation, Alex Garland having been born in 1970.

13. As we begin to see this hint of romance between the softening Selena and Jim, I'd ask readers to consider how well this story would have been received by its dominant audience had Selena been white and Jim black. Would the young white males who predominated among fans who embraced a fantasy with themselves as Jim, getting next to the pretty young black woman in the post-apocalyptic scenario, have likewise as enthusiastically embraced a story in which the sex-gender polarity were reversed? If not, why?

Selena and her companions have reached the roadblock designated in the radio broadcast, whereupon Frank, the "father" of this little group, is infected by a drop of blood from a corpse. Just as Selena is screaming at the reluctant Jim to kill Frank, and just as Jim is about to do the deed, a flurry of shots from unseen assault rifles riddle Frank's body. The soldiers are here, and they transport the grief-stricken Hannah, Selena, and Jim back to their base—a converted palatial estate—where they are met by their new "father," Major Henry West. West greets them with an incongruously light-hearted welcome, considering they've just lost their beloved Frank, and once they've settled in and begun taking showers, we see the soldiers—in an ominous foreshadowing of the group's new danger—taunting one of their more effeminate comrades (the cook, who wears a frilly apron, and is called "a fucking Doris") by playing stupid, reckless games with Frank's car. A sense of that frat-boy threat that women know only too well.

Selena's character, after her transformative softening at the idyllic campsite, becomes even more vulnerable now, crying to Jim in despair over Hannah's grief, showing us how Selena is being transformed, with Frank dead now, into Hannah's mother.

In a scene immediately following a defensive "battle" against an assault by a herd of "the infected," which pumps up the saurian hyper-macho Corporal Mitchell, Mitchell re-enters the building, and in a scene dripping with that feral locker-room innuendo, disarms Selena, taking her machete and using it to balefully mime his own erect penis. It is now that we realize Selena and Hannah are about to become Damsels in Distress.

After the symbolic disarming and threat of rape, Major West—read: the bad father—takes newly-adopted son, Jim, to the side to explain that the radio message was meant to gather women as sex slaves for the soldiers. So Selena's development, if we track it here, is from survivalist soldier and leader, to daughter, to mother, to Damsel in Distress. Just as importantly, this transformation of Selena serves the film's overall purpose not in showing Selena's development, but in *giving Jim his chance to become the new father*.

Jim is locked up with the rebellious Sergeant Farrell, who informs Jim that West is crazy as the proverbial "shithouse rat,"[14] and that Great Britain has been quarantined—that the virus has not, as earlier believed, destroyed all of human civilization.

14. From the methane? IDK.

Farrell and Jim are to be taken to a killing ground and shot by the vicious Corporal Mitchell and another soldier. When Mitchell's comrade shoots Farrell, depriving Mitchell of the sadistic satisfaction of bayonetting Farrell, who Mitchell hates, Mitchell attacks his comrade, and Jim takes advantage of the momentary confusion to make his escape by diving into a hillside of putrid corpses.

Golgotha.

Place of the Skull.

Then comes a resurrection scene . . . but not for a Prince of Peace.

Jim hides in a pile of corpses, and when his former captors aren't looking, he "rises from the dead," whereupon he sees a plane fly over, confirming Farrell's story. Jim is now transformed, ironically by love, into a steely-eyed fighter, and a pathetic fallacy rainstorm accompanies him half naked, ripped and stained, marching through the elements toward rescue and retribution.

Selena and Hannah, meanwhile, are being dressed up by the soldiers in preparation for being sexually broken in by their captors. Selena, the former and formidable zombie-fighter, is now disarmed, though not without a new kind of (feminine) agency. She promises to sexually cooperate if the soldiers leave her alone with Hannah for a bit, and she gives Hannah a fistful of valium. Hannah asks if she is trying to kill her, and Selena says, no—as a good mother who is doing the best she can for her daughter, she explains, "I'm making it so you don't care."[15]

As we approach the climax of the film, Jim is sounding the siren at the roadblock, calling out West and his soldiers for a jungle fight, just as Selena and Hannah are being prepared for their first gang rape. Jim is no longer the former bike messenger, nor is he the gentle counterpoint to Selena's stone-cold warrior. These roles are now flipped, as Jim is transformed into a Man—determined and deadly—and he has acquired . . . of course . . . a gun. He kills one soldier at the roadblock, then returns and releases a captive zombie to run amok in the palace,[16] and as the soldiers are picked off by

15. As an aside, I have to say that, even though Hannah was not as prominent a character as Selena, in many respects she accidentally became the most "feminist" character. She was not over-manipulated by a male writer and director into being a man's idea of a feminist character (killer, therefore "honorary male"). Hannah is rational, decisive when she needs to be, fearless, and plays a somewhat comedic scene as the stoned concubine-to-be who spooks her captors with speculations that their companions are all dead.

16. By shooting a chain in two—another trope, Shoot the Lock Off, which, for anyone who has tried it, is nearly impossible except at point blank range, where it then jeopardizes the shooter from ricochet and flak.

infection, Jim advances toward his confrontation with chief rapist, Mitchell. The transformed Jim drops down out of a skylight, bashes Mitchell's head against a wall, then—in a state of righteous Rage (yes)—Jim kills the odious Mitchell by gouging out his eyes with bare hands. Jim, in an Oedipal struggle, has displaced West as the father, and won the two women.

A final escape scene ensues. West, conveniently offscreen for three scenes, reappears (Not Dead Yet trope) to shoot and wound Jim (and Hannah gets rid of West by driving him with the car into the arms of a rage-zombie). We are then transported to an idyllic cottage in the country, where Jim is the (wounded) dad, Selena is the (nurturing) mom, and Hannah is the (cheerful) daughter. The world has been restored to a microcosmic (gender) order.

A plane flies over and spots their ground signal, which we saw Selena making—Olde Tyme mom style—*at a sewing machine.*

Just as this writer's generation was caught between its normative inheritance from the generations before it, the social tumult into which it was born, and the fragmented moral pluralism of the 1990s and turn of the century, this is another film that reflects a clumsy reaching for some feminist sensibility by men who think they know more about feminism than they do.

A white man generates, albeit with a few minor transgressions, a white man's fantasy of a feminist "honorary male" (in extremis), and resolves his plot by returning to the normative gender order, the man coming into his own through redemptive violence, and Getting the (now male-protected) Girl(s).

All in all, from a critical, not ethical, point of view, a pretty valuable movie, and well done.

6

Monstrous Women and the Idol of Success: Karen Crowder

MELISSA SILVERSTEIN:

> Tilda Swinton, superb in *Michael Clayton*, makes a virtue of being the only gal in her own otherwise male-dominated ensemble. Her performance as the morally decentered opposition lawyer Karen Crowder is a brilliant reproach to a frankly wretched part: the role is tinged with misogyny, but Swinton makes Karen, with all her neurosis and terror, seem like the stricken victim of a man's world.[1]

I agree with Silverstein. *Michael Clayton* is partially redeemed by Tilda Swinton's performance from the clueless misogyny of its own writer, director, and producers; because Swinton takes a Monstrous Female and humanizes her in a way that bridges—in my view—the contradictions of a film like this and the contradictions of women in the real world contesting for the traditional power of men. When I saw Swinton's "Karen Crowder," I found myself empathizing with her even in the face of her murderous calculations. I thought of the real Hillary Clinton, not the persona she has been driven by her ambition to project in public for so many years, but the more tragic private one—obsessive, perpetually worried, terrified of any whiff of vulnerability being discovered, and thereby cut off from the kind of vulnerability that is the precondition of intimacy. Sacrificing all before the idol of success.[2]

1. Silverstein, *Women & Hollywood.*

2. Film that portrays this idolatry in *men* tends to redeem the male protagonist from his personal failures by making him very good at his job. Perhaps what will redeem films is when they can portray this idolatry in men the same way they did for Karen Crowder. But, as it stands in this film, Michael Clayton—also a failure in personal matters—is

Karen Crowder is not the main character in *Michael Clayton*, Michael is, played by George Clooney. Along with Arthur Eden, the brilliant, bipolar attorney at the mega-firm that employs Michael as its fixer. Michael is "fixing" the problem of Arthur going off the rails as lead attorney defending U-North (a kind of fictionalized Monsanto) in a class-action law suit over a highly carcinogenic herbicide. Karen Crowder is U-North's General Counsel, a position that we can infer is relatively new, and relatively tentative, given her obvious anxiety and obsequiousness in the company of her boss, CEO Don Jeffries, and her embarrassed reference to a bumpy start in the not-too-distant past.

Karen Crowder is not the main character in this film, but she is the main *villain*. She organizes a contract killing of Arthur, followed by an attempted assassination of Michael Clayton, to neutralize the threat of her employer losing its multibillion-dollar class-action lawsuit.

In a sense, I am departing from the theme of honorary male with Karen Crowder, because—even apart from the casual misogyny of the film—Tilda Swinton's performance hits inadvertently on a paradoxical truth about real women trying to make it as honorary men in the real world of high-powered politics and business. If it degrades men, it will degrade women. But that is not what this film is meant to convey, at least by intent.

Let's talk about misogyny first.

The writer and director, Tony Gilroy, is the author of the screenplays for the *Bourne* series, high-powered, fast-action thrillers starring Matt Damon as the amnesiac former government assassin, Jason Bourne. Gilroy was nominated for an Academy Award for *Michael Clayton*, as were others; but his comfort zone is obviously with the boys; and his one female action lead was actually Jen, in *Star Wars: Rogue One*, which he co-wrote with Chris Weitz and Gareth Edwards. Jen was a Smurfette, the only significant female part in an otherwise all-male film. Jen kicked ass, for sure, and she was "hot."

---

stereotypically redeemed in the public/professional world by solving the whodunit and taking down Crowder. Swinton's portrayal *does* make Karen Crowder come across as a *victim*, which I will argue is the truth in many respects about what happens to women trying to "make it" as honorary men—the moral hazard of "equality" in a world where men have the prerogative, even the obligation, to engage in cutthroat competition. However, the film goes on to subvert Swinton's performance, and its implications, by depicting *Crowder*, and not patriarchal cutthroat competition, as somehow monstrous.

Michael Clayton centers its initial action around the manic monologue of Arthur Eden, after his middle-aged infatuation with Anna, a nineteen-year-old member of one of the plaintiff families, triggers a man-epiphany about the depth of the evil of the company he represents. This is the Insider Becomes Outsider trope. Arthur's monologue opens the film as a voice-over, then the movie circles around to re-capture that monologue again in person after Arthur is locked up for stripping naked at Anna's deposition. During this carpet-chewing monologue, Arthur describes his Damascene moment, which happened while he was with two prostituted Lithuanian women. Understand, that Arthur is meant to be the absolute most sympathetic character in the whole film;[3] and this is important, because as he describes this epiphany—after he has understood the difference between Good and Evil—he says:

> I look up and there's Marty in my office. He's got some champagne. He tells me we just hit 30,000 billable hours on U-North and he wants to celebrate. So an hour later, I find myself in a whorehouse in Chelsea with two Lithuanian redheads taking turns sucking my dick. I'm laying there and I'm trying not to come and I wanna . . . I wanna make it last, so I start doing the math. I think, "Thirty thousand hours, what is that? That's 24 times 30. That's 720 hours in a month, 8760 hours in a year . . . No, wait, wait, wait! Because it's years! It's lives! And the numbers are making me dizzy and, you know . . . now, instead of trying not to come, I'm trying not to think, and I can't stop. I mean, is this me? Am I this freak organism that has been sent here to sleep and eat . . . and defend this one horrific chain of carcinogenic molecules? Is that my destiny? Is that my fate? Is that it, Michael? Is that my grail? Two Lithuanian mouths on my cock? Is that the correct answer to the multiple choice of me?

I'll wager that this monologue strikes men and women differently. I'll further wager that many men will feel himpathy for Arthur without giving much thought to how thoughtlessly he has simultaneously objectified and marginalized two probable victims of sex trafficking[4] whom he has exploited with none of the remorse he now feels for defending his client. Two women whom he reduces without a second thought to two *mouths* on *his* cock, and is that *his* destiny, *his* grail, the answer to the multiple choice of *him*. Because as we identify with Arthur, in his moment of revelation,

3. A trope that Kate Mann calls "himpathy."

4. "It's lives!" But there are two Lithuanian women whose lives are incidental.

we know that it is all about Me. Man-Me. Those exploited women who have been ordered by a pimp to stick Arthur's rich, middle-aged dick in their mouths are not the equivalent of (virginal) nineteen-year-old Anna, the Midwestern farm girl who has stolen Arthur's heart—"God's perfect little creature," Arthur calls her—and inaugurated his redemption. Two throwaway Lithuanian "redheads" are just part of Arthur's symbolic background music, Arthur's account of probable rape[5] being kind of funny and cute. Another "cute" throwaway line is Michael himself, on the phone with another attorney, saying, "Look, what can I say? Don't piss off a motivated stripper." Whore-Madonna, anyone?

The Monstrous Feminine takes a turn with Karen Crowder. Generally speaking, the term, as coined by Barbara Creed,[6] refers to men's sexual anxieties with regard to women, to toothy vaginas and castration complexes. But with Crowder, who is systematically de-sexualized in the film, her monstrosity is based on her inability to *handle* man-stuff in a man's world without resorting to the worst of the man's world, in this case contract killing through a shadowy Blackwater-type security agency. So when one *man*, Arthur Eden, suddenly faces a moral dilemma and tries to put justice aright (albeit by breaking his oath as a lawyer) for the virginal nineteen-year-old Anna and her family, it is *the woman* Karen Crowder's inability to deal with the crisis that leads her to a fatal escalation—which, by the way, will be put aright by another *man* who comes face to face with his own moral dilemma—Michael Clayton (joining the Insider Becomes Outsider trope).

Crowder's de-sexualization—accomplished with unflattering shots of her rubbing her sweaty armpits and non-provocatively half dressed in a hotel room, emphasizing rolls of fat along her midsection, dressed for work in suits that efface any hint of sexuality—highlights her loss of (sexually attractive) womanhood (in the mind of the writer-director) as she attempts to make it in the world of real (ruthlessly competitive) men.[7]

5. Department of State, "Lithuania." More than forty percent of people trafficked from Lithuania are women and girls destined for the sex trade, mostly in Britain and the United States. These women are under the constant control of pimps, "broken in" by gang rape, often at the ages of fourteen to fifteen, and "work" virtually as sex slaves. Therefore, anyone who pays (ultimately pays a pimp) to have sex with them is engaging in nonconsensual sex, i.e., rape. This condition of coerced servitude is true of *most* prostituted women, and should give pause to the people who try to sanitize this situation by calling prostitution "sex work," and try to pass off this vicious and highly-organized form of sexual exploitation as a "contractual" relation.

6. And seen through a Freudian-Lacanian frame, again.

7. There is a whole field of psychology, called "disgust psychology," studying how

Her loss of womanhood, in contrast to the fair Anna, is precisely the basis of her monstrosity, *monster* in its meaning as something that deviates from the norm.[8]

> Crowder's "unexcused" incompetence raises the damning possibility that women per se may be ill-suited for the world of high-powered lawyers. This is a more troubling conclusion than other lawyer films that imply women can be competent lawyers if they reconcile the inherent tensions between their professional and personal lives. Karen Crowder epitomizes the depravity that exists once women venture from the private sphere, where they are thought to find their ultimate satisfaction, into the public sphere of the legal world. Stripped of her femininity, she is a shell of a human being with no sense of purpose, no significant personal relationships, and no redeeming personal traits. Whereas being a workaholic can be seen as a sign of passion and dedication in a man, in a woman it is portrayed as a sign of weakness. With no sense of self, she looks to other people for answers, for confirmation of her role and identity. With her entire identity defined by her performance as general counsel of U-North, Crowder does the unthinkable [contract killing].[9]

Karen Crowder becomes simultaneously the antithesis of both sweet Anna and the Hot Chick with a Gun (redeemed, at least, by fuckability).[10]

---

disgust is learned as a social *policing* mechanism. Who is in? Who is out? There is a long history of hatred for the female body, sexualized and de-sexualized, reinforced by culturally encoded disgust. This exists alongside the idealization and sexualization of women's bodies—which are infantilized with compulsory hairlessness and thinness, demobilized in high heels, and silenced in representation (with its opposites represented as disgusting). The body's boundaries are policed by socialized disgust; and women's bodies, as the boundaries that are breached, by menstruation, lactation, and childbirth, are represented as disgusting objects. This body-boundary disgust is symbolically associated with something called "animal-reminder disgust," which is likewise associated with the fear of death. Culturally, the object of disgust is dealt with by expulsion, often using a scapegoat mechanism. The object of disgust is expelled from within the social boundary, exiled or destroyed. Karen Crowder will eventually be destroyed figuratively (as she collapses to the floor) and expelled (arrested and presumably sent to prison), this being the cathartic moment in the film.

8. Monstrosity for females comes in several guises: castrator, bad mother, black widow, ambitious woman, etc. Mythically, monsters are often "unnatural" hybrids—centaurs, minotaurs, etc. Androgyny, the manifestation of both "masculine" and "feminine" characteristics, is still perceived by many as monstrous, or "unnaturally" hybrid.

9. Banks, "Women Lawyers Betrayed," 119.

10. The criterion of "fuckability," reviewing now, is related to the maintenance of

Her character is an expression of men's sense of dislocation in the face of women with economic and political power. This male discomfort extends far back into literary history. Just look at Chaucer and Shakespeare (unreformulated by decontextualized modern readings), when the monstrosity of women in power was codified in philosophy and law, and this same trope re-emerging in Michael Clayton is as unsurprising as men's casual acceptance of the story line and the narrative's casual misogyny.

> The distorted image of women lawyers in film is fairly widespread and is the subject of frequent commentary. Most women lawyers in 1980s and 1990s films are unmarried or divorced, struggling to reconcile their professional lives with their personal lives . . . The prevalent theme in these films is that women cannot exist in the legal world without sacrificing their "female self"—their roles as mother, daughter, wife, or *girl*friend.[11]

Compare this with the spate of popular ruthless (black!) women-in-power series that now dominates the television scene (*How to Get Away with Murder*, *Scandal*), and we can gain a glimpse of three different, related phenomena: how reactionary Karen Crowder's character is, how popular race and gender decoys can conceal actual power structures, and how modernity's moral anchor, stretching its line back into the past, has broken loose and left us ethically adrift. In *Murder* and *Scandal*, two different but both brilliant professional black women—both trained as lawyers—are portrayed as successfully playing hardball with the Big Boys, amorally and ruthlessly so, each with a multi-racial, sexually-diverse posse, who bang their ways through hyperactive, life-and-death plot twists with the alacrity of Serena Williams knifing back fast serves at the Australian Open. Annalise Keating (Viola Davis) and Olivia Pope (Kerry Washington), characters created by a very successful African American woman—Shonda Rhimes—represent black women who have "made it," albeit at the expense of nearly all remaining moral ground (a postmodern conceit), in ways that look remarkably post-racial and post-feminist (both characters are highly

men's sexual prerogative, a perceived entitlement to women's bodies, and an entitlement to define women as sexual objects, particularly in the face of women's "incursions" into formerly male fields apart from sex, like certain work and sports. It is a way in which men can continue to "enclose" women, reducing them to a figuratively possessable object. Where men are seeing their control over women diminished in other fields, they will more aggressively reassert that control in the sexual realm. You can have that gun in my story, as long as you meet my "hotness" standard.

11. Ibid.

sexualized; and both series use a good deal of fast and furious sex involving almost all the main characters to salaciously retain their tempo). In the real world of the audience, however, the majority of racial minorities and/or women are still getting the shitty end of the stick.

This is classic race-gender decoy signaling (falsely) that if you work hard (and set aside any moral scruples) you can make it (in the white "meritocracy"). It abandons any and all criticism of the actual system within which these women are "succeeding." This, in turn, indicts our "post-theoretical," post-modern period. Old moral strictures held on through the evolution of a political economy based on avarice and ruthlessness, waning vestiges of some long-forgotten attachment to actual human virtues. Now they are being discarded in favor of raw power, and that raw power is celebrated as virtue; just as symbolism (underdogs "making it") comes to trump reality: unreconstructed racial and gender inequality created and maintained by the very system within which that inequality nests.

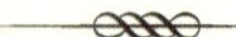

Karen Crowder is meant as a warning from men to women, an old fashioned one that predates the MTV kick-and-punch narrative pace and post-Tarantino moral destitution of *Scandal* and *Murder*. It says that at the end of *gender*, as a system that divides power between men and women, is chaos and horror. In a very real sense, *Michael Clayton* is a 1970s Reluctant Hero trope,[12] and women are seen through that (male) lens. This is why the predominantly old, white, male Academy of Motion Picture Arts and Sciences was quick to bestow multiple Oscar nominations on the film. It was familiar: film *noir* (concrete jungle), hero-lawyer (male), Insider Becomes Outsider (male), Western (white male, reluctant hero). This is why many of us *enjoyed* the film with our first uncritical viewing. The conventions were familiar, the production values high, and we like those things for the same reason I can eat a large bag of Twizzlers—they're tasty, strangely addictive and familiar satisfactions without much nutrition.

Katarzyna Poloczek makes some interesting observations about *Michael Clayton* and Karen Crowder in her essay, "From the Kitchen into the Bathroom."[13] Women characters, prior to the backlash against feminism, were portrayed in the kitchen: the Angel in the Kitchen trope. Think *I Love*

12. Kamir, "Michael Clayton," para. 23.

13. Poloczek, "From the Kitchen to the Bathroom."

Lucy, *Leave it to Beaver*, *Little House on the Prairie*, and more recently *Soul Food*. Poloczek notes that as women were confronted (in the male mind) with the drawbacks of feminism, the site of their angst became the bathroom. She cites episodes of *House*, *Black Swan*, and *Michael Clayton*.

In Michael Clayton, this happens in the first scene after the opening sequence in which Michael's car is mysteriously blown up. We flash back. On screen: "Four days earlier." We are in the swarming hive of the big law firm, "Kenner, Back & Ledeen." One lawyer approaches another with a telephone, announcing, "It's that cunt from the Wall Street Journal," whereupon his Big Boss takes this unseen but uppity "cunt" and puts her quickly and soundly in her place. That's what the "cunt" gets for playing with the Big Boys. The next thing the boss asks, during a frantic midnight crisis management scene in the Big Office, is, "Where in the fuck is Karen Crowder?" Her name called, Karen does not make her entrance in the film with the protagonist's first-scene backlighting. Instead, we find her cowering in a bathroom stall, mouth agape, overwhelmed with anxiety, lifting up her arm and showing the audience a huge sweat stain that would have been covered by her suit jacket.

> Likewise, throughout the rest of the film, the official game of (self) deception that the Swinton character plays is interrupted and undermined mainly in the *bathroom* scenes where the nearly out-of-her-mind woman puts aside her professional mask, and we can discern her true emotions. Unseen and unjudged by others, it is only in the bathroom that Crowder can be in touch with her body and her real feelings. Karen escapes to the bathroom each time when the situation becomes too overwhelming and when she is about to lose control. The audience examines Karen's exposed body, with all its imperfections, corporeal fluids, and strained nerves when her entire organism revolts against what her mind is rationalizing.[14]

Paradoxically, these are the most compelling scenes in the film, in my opinion. In spite of the male misogyny that permeated this film and motivated her scenes, Swinton humanized them with her amazing performance. They confront us with a reality for women trying to make it in a "man's world" that is difficult to acknowledge without setting the stage for certain ideological confusions. This is where I think we can usefully

14. Ibid.

compare the fictional character of Karen Crowder with the real politician, Hillary Clinton.

Managing a public persona, especially for people driven by powerful ambitions, requires the most profound kind of compartmentalization—the separating out of one's performances, even one's professional duties and obligations, from all other aspects of one's life that might be categorized as personal. There is no more emblematic role for compartmentalizing than that of the combat soldier, who might engage in the most barbarous kinds of violence and calculated cruelty in a war zone, then be expected to behave in dramatically different ways as a brother, husband, or father.[15]

In an interview, Tilda Swinton explained how she got into character for Karen Crowder, saying, "For me, she is like a soldier. She wears a uniform. She follows the flag. It is reductive to think this is only about lawyers or America. It's about systems that require people to leave themselves outside while following orders." Swinton went on to describe Crowder as a "good girl" who wanted to do a good job, but in her need to prove herself surrendered to desperate measures. "My lawyer was at the screening . . ." said Swinton, "and I said to her, 'Tell me this isn't true.' And she said, 'Well, I believe it.'"[16]

Hillary Clinton began running for the presidency of the United States sometime between 1992 and 2000. We can't read her mind about exactly when she set her cap for it;[17] but in 2000, she changed her address to New York for the express purpose of using her and former President Clinton's political capital to run for the safe, soon-to-be vacated US Senate seat of Daniel Patrick Moynihan. Few people doubt that this move was calculated as the logical springboard for an eventual presidential run, or she'd have run for Senate in Arkansas. When she did run in 2008, her willingness to perform in accordance with the cynical machinations of several of her husband's former managers (winning her a reputation as a highly scripted, and even wooden candidate) backfired in South Carolina, and set Barack Obama on a course to defeat her for the nomination. Her consolation prize was to be appointed Secretary of State, whereupon she very predictably threw her hat back into the ring for 2016. What was going to be a party

15. Real combat soldiers are overwhelmingly men. The same applies, however, to sisters, wives, and mothers in armed service.

16. Wloszczyna, "'Clayton' revives conspiracy genre," para. 27–28.

17. Carroll, "10 times." She stated in 1994 that she wanted to be the President, then played it off as a joke. By 2006, she admitted she was "looking at it."

coronation ran into a roadblock as a populist revolt threw up Bernie Sanders, an avowed "democratic socialist," as a serious primary opponent. The rest, we know, is history, as she was narrowly and stunningly defeated by the unlikely, terrifyingly stupid, and dimly venal Donald Trump.

Politics is gendered, and when anyone is running for President, the highly gendered question is raised, again and again, of who is tough enough (read: macho enough) to be a "strong Commander-in-Chief." Clinton knew this, and as a Senator, she was already erring on the side of military action, voting yes on every military action proposed, including the disastrous war in Iraq. As Secretary of State, she hawkishly promoted the expansion of US attacks from two to seven nations, the (again disastrous) overthrow of Libya by military action, and even facilitating a *coup d'etat* against a democratic government in Honduras. No one was going to out-macho her as Commander-in-Chief; and she amassed a body count to prove it.

Like Karen Crowder, though, where men could get away with doing these amoral man things in the tough "man's world," women were caught in a double-bind. On the one hand, when you commit big crimes, you deserve to be punished; and both women were willing to have others killed to get where they wanted to be. On the other hand—and this recalls the contradictions of the O. J. Simpson trial—the public sphere is infected with sexism (and racism), and there is little doubt that the difference between the way Clinton was treated for doing the same things that men had done was—for a substantial part of the population—based on a profound double-standard. So, for some the opposition to Clinton during the nomination process was based on opposition to particular policies that were similarly opposed in their male guises by Bush and Obama. For others, there was explicit sexism. And so many people found themselves simultaneously opposing Clinton's policies while trying to defend her from attacks that were based on sexism, as well as defend themselves from those who took any opposition to Clinton as evidence that they were guilty of sexism.

In the film, *Michael Clayton*, speaking for myself, I had a glimpse, through Swinton's portrayal, of the special price paid by women for that kind of ambition—and I felt empathy for the character as she rehearsed and rehearsed, fighting always with a kind of latent self-loathing at a perceived inadequacy drilled into a woman for her lifetime, lapsing into a terrible sadness between "takes" on her upcoming performance in that bathroom mirror. And it makes me wonder about Clinton, in her moments of highly privatized vulnerability, and how unbearably sad she may actually be. Justice aside, because I'm not clean either. I was a combat soldier; and I committed brutal actions in pursuit of my own ambition to prove some version of masculinity.

The danger here, in acknowledging the moral and emotional cost for women who are trying to fill what were formerly male shoes, is twofold. First, by focusing on the cost for women, we might miss what is wrong with these forms of power in the first place;[18] and second is that anti-feminists will be quick to attempt, as Poloczek points out, laying this issue at the feet of feminism for "taking women out of their proper roles," emboldening the anti-feminist backlash.

Has Hillary Clinton made herself over to be an honorary male as a route to the top? I would suggest the answer is a qualified yes. Traditionally male roles do not adapt themselves—or their "masculine" character—to liberal feminists. The liberal feminist, if her goal is to "make it" in the existing hierarchies, will be forced to adapt herself to the norms, goals, and attitudes of the job description, developed by foregoing patriarchal males within a meshwork of patriarchal social relations, some pregnant with violence.

A related problem is the "cult of success." For Christians, who follow an itinerant beggar rabbi who was killed by the authorities, the notion of meritocracy, and its "cult of success," ought to be anathema. Moreover, the "cult of success" mindset is one that easily substitutes individual and symbolic success stories for the goal of systemic justice (for all). It is a powerful temptation, because any group of people who have been systematically put down by being told how they are unfit to "make it" will understandably celebrate anyone who proves this particular claim of unfitness wrong—simultaneously rebelling against the system while accepting and reiterating its basic premises.

Hillary Clinton did make it, even if she didn't make it to the very top. And while I wonder about the price she paid, morally and emotionally, to get there, I would ask the same question of the men who preceded her. Recognizing that her status as a woman really *was* an impediment in a sexist society, I also have to recognize that the price she paid may have been steeper than the price paid by men. In real life, I imagine this is very difficult for her. Clinton did engage in directed violence, though unlike Karen Crowder, who is represented as pursuing violent goals for personal gain, Clinton—like all politicians—wrapped her violence in the flag and

18. Or the fact that men are, likewise, emotionally *damaged* by masculinity.

characterized it as *redemptive*. In real life, it is true, she continues to benefit from her status and power; but I wonder if she might also be sad in her center.

Karen Crowder, on the other hand, must be made to pay.

> Ironically, now as a converted neophyte, Clayton executes the conclusive justice on Karen . . . Clayton triumphantly and patronizingly preaches Crowder a backlash lesson . . . "For such a smart person, you really are lost, aren't you?" . . . Swinton's character seems to epitomize aptly . . . the recent backlash against women. Ingenious as the acting performance is, it does maintain the negative stereotypes of professional women clichés: Crowder [note the surname, *crowding* in where she does not belong] is viewed as desperate; an emotionally disturbed person with no personal life who decided to build her career over the dead bodies of her competitors—not just for money or power but to prove to men that she "can have it all." She is ultimately overcome and victimized by the very same patriarchal system that she tried to serve so dutifully.[19]

19. Poloczek, "From the Kitchen to the Bathroom," 231.

7

Bad Rape, Good Rape: Lisbeth Salander

THE *MILLENNIUM TRILOGY* WAS authored by Stieg Larsson, who died shortly after the third novel was published. In the Anglophone world, the first in the trilogy was titled *The Girl with the Dragon Tattoo*. The trilogy features Lisbeth Salander, a tiny, tough, cyber-punk hacker with an eidetic memory, as its unlikely heroine. The film we will review here is the American version of the first novel, also named *The Girl with the Dragon Tattoo*, in which Lisbeth Salander is played by Roonie Mara, and the other principle character, Mikael Blomkvist, is played by Daniel Craig.

Dragon Tattoo, directed by David Fincher (*Alien 3*, *Seven*, *Fight Club*, *Zodiac*, *Gone Girl*), was a box office and critical success in 2011, though not a blockbuster. Fincher likes *dark* in his movies, and *Dragon Tattoo* had that. The film is well-acted, well-edited, with edge-of-your-seat pacing. And it is definitely being touted as a feminist masterpiece in some quarters, even though it was written by a man, scripted by a man, and directed by a man—who, by the way, in the film makes the man, who was secondary to the plot in the book, more or less the principle character whose point of view is primarily represented.

I am not saying men cannot write books or direct films that have feminist sensibilities; I am saying that *this* director, when you look at his CV and what he has done to alter the book for *Dragon Tattoo*, is a boy's director.

The story is a whodunit set in Sweden. A fourteen year old girl—Harriet Vanger, from an obscenely wealthy, corrupt, and Nazi-sympathetic family—disappeared decades ago, and an investigative reporter, Mikael "Kalle" Blomkvist—back on his heels from losing a serious lawsuit—is hired by the family's aging patriarch, Henrik Vanger, Harriet's great uncle, to find out who murdered her. A parallel story is Lisbeth's.[1]

In *Dragon Tattoo*, we are introduced to Lisbeth as a contract researcher for the giant Milton Security firm, where she employs her hacking skills and eidetic memory to compile profiles of people, which include a certain number of illegal forays into their personal and professional computers. She shows up for work on her motorcycle, a black-clad goth-cyberpunk, multiply pierced and tattooed, hair slashed and spiked, with vampire make-up. Many have speculated that she is autistic; but for those familiar with her whole story, we know that her unusual responses to social situations and her peculiar, if heterodox, moral intensity, are outgrowths of long childhood experience of paternal and institutional abuse. As the story begins, she is still counted as a psychiatric ward of the state who reports to an officially appointed guardian.

Before Lisbeth is recruited by Blomkvist to assist him in his investigation, her state-sanctioned ward—with whom she had established a decent human relationship, and who lets her live autonomously—suffers a massive stroke, whereupon she is paired with a new legal guardian: Nils Bjurman, a sexual predator who coerces Lisbeth into oral sex in his office in exchange for enough money to fix her broken computer.

When the computer was broken, a purse snatcher had grabbed her backpack in the subway, whereupon she trashed her assailant, revealing to audiences what readers already knew, that Lisbeth, in spite of being less than five feet tall, is a wiry kickboxer. In fact, her fighting skills, her eidetic memory, and her hacking skills (which are a kind of x-ray vision), have been interpreted by some critics as making Lisbeth almost a punk-noir super-hero.

Lisbeth sets a trap for Bjurman by installing a video recorder in her bag, then going to his house to again exchange oral sex for a check—intending to blackmail him with the video to checkmate his control and advances. This backfires when Bjurman brutally beats her, ties her down, and sodomizes her. When Bjurman releases her, he behaves as if they have just had a consensual encounter, even offering her a ride home.

Lisbeth limps home, badly beaten, with a video of the rape.

1. In the books, the line of continuity between each installment of the trilogy is *Lisbeth's* story, which emerges more clearly in conjunction with other investigations; but in *Dragon Tattoo*, the American film, her peculiar individuality is more important than the story that has formed her character, and the male lead is more central than Lisbeth.

The next time she returns to Bjurman's, she immediately disables him with a stun gun, and in a cathartic revenge scene where she is wearing a kind of spooky war-paint make-up, ties him up, gags him with duct tape, kicks the hell out of him, anally rapes him with a large dildo, and tattoos "I am a sadistic pig a pervert and a rapist" on his chest. She further informs the now-petrified and broken Bjurman that he will give her access to her own money and write regular and laudatory reports on her "progress" without ever seeing her . . . or she will kill him.

Through Vanger's lawyer, Blomkvist meets Lisbeth—who has investigated Blomkvist for Vanger—and Blomkvist hires her as his research assistant. Between the two of them, the investigation of the "murder" of Harriet leads them to believe that Harriet was on the trail of a psychotic murderer of women. In a sense, then, this film has everything: cathartic revenge, an intrepid investigative journalist, a super-heroine, Nazis, and a serial killer.

Early on in their association, Lisbeth climbs into bed with Blomkvist. Blomkvist appears to be irresistible to pretty much every woman he meets, and this is true in the books as well, perhaps a fantasy of Larsson himself. Lisbeth herself is pansexual, having a female lover as well who we get glimpses of early in the film, but who disappears after serving her titillating purpose.[2]

As Blomkvist and Salander zero in on the serial killer—who they believe is responsible for Harriet's disappearance—Blomkvist comes face-to-face with the killer in a vulnerable situation. It is Martin, Harriet's brother, who captures Blomkvist and is in the process of torturing him to death when Lisbeth, alerted to Blomkvist's peril, shows up just in time to take Martin out with a golf club and save Blomkvist. The gravely injured Martin slips off, gets in his car to effect a getaway, pursued now by an armed Lisbeth on her motorcycle, whereupon he crashes the car and is burned to death in the resulting inferno, as Lisbeth looks on with grisly satisfaction.

This is a five-act film, instead of the standard three, so after the climax, there is a lengthy wind-down before the denouement. Harriet hasn't been killed after all, and had actually escaped, so Blomkvist tracks her down. Lisbeth hacks the uber-rich plaintiff who sued Blomkvist and transfers something like a billion dollars of his money to her secret Cayman account—making her an insanely wealthy super-hero. Lisbeth, who is now in love with the polyamorous Blomkvist, rides over to give him an expensive

2. In the books, her name is Miriam Wu, and she plays a minor but significant role in the second and third books.

jacket bought with her (justifiably, in the context of the film) ill-gotten gain and sees him with his long-time (married) lover and colleague, Erica Berger, whereupon Lisbeth throws the gift in the dumpster and rides off into her bitter disillusionment.

Larsson stated more than once before his death that the trilogy was about the abuse of women by men. Larsson said he was motivated all his life by guilt, after having witnessed a girl being gang raped by his friends, after which he did nothing. The first book is about the sexual exploitation and rape of Lisbeth, as well as the sexual abuse and murder of women; the second revolves around a sex-trafficking investigation; and the third highlights the difficulties Lisbeth faces—as a woman—in pleading her cases before a patriarchally biased legal system. Larsson was, in his own mind, trying to practice a feminist sensibility, though I hope to make the case that he was only partially successful; and that what he did accomplish was further watered down by David Fincher's film.

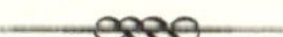

The first thing calling for a closer analysis here is rape.

There is a popular saying that "rape is not about sex, but about power." For reasons I will explain in depth in the last chapter, this is an invalid claim. There are many controlling and even abusive, violent behaviors that are not sexual and not rape. What defines rape *is* its sexual aspect. Men *are* sexually aroused when they commit rape. So while what they are doing is about domination and control, it is also inescapably *sexual*. Actual sex in the real world is not separable from power—in the case of rape, violent coercive power. Aggression, hostility, control, and the desire to humiliate are *routinely* eroticized.

The subtext of the lie that rape is not about sex is that "real" sex involves affection; but the reality is that a great deal of actual sexual activity is exploitative, instrumental, objectifying, fetishized, and even hostile—even in many heterosexual marriages. A common complaint of many wives is that they feel pressured to have sex, or to do things during sex they do not desire.[3] I have heard men, even liberal men, talk about "hate-fucking" unpopular female public figures like Sarah Palin or Ann Coulter.[4]

3. Often stimulated in men's minds by what they've observed in pornography.

4. Because sex is seen as punishment, again showing how sex and hostility can and do intersect at the same coordinates.

Rape associates sex with hostility, aggression, and even revenge. Many people who claim to oppose rape, however, are more than willing to celebrate the potential for unlikeable male convicts being raped in prison as a form of social revenge.

So *the association between hostility and sex* that defines rape culture has been assimilated by the same culture that claims to censure rape.

This is what I found most troublesome in *Girl with the Dragon Tattoo*. The audience is invited by the narrative flow to enjoy the revenge rape of a rapist as a form or justice, which, while it may have a kind of juridical symmetry, reinforces the underlying idea that sex is associated with hostility (a doer and a done-to), and is seen as a legitimate means of social control—the Prison as Punitive Rape Camp notion.

Well. Guess what.

This is precisely how actual rape functions illegitimately in male-dominant society. The threat of rape keeps women in their places. The threat of rape (in prison) can be used to keep Bad Men in their places. Sex plus hostility equals rape culture.

"Capital punishment is the state killing people to show that killing people is wrong." Remember that bumper sticker? Revenge rape is raping people to show that raping people is wrong. Pay attention, in all stories where violence redeems, to how the plot is contrived to lead the audience—often via one-dimensionally bad characters who "have it coming"—into enthusiastic participation in the violence as cathartic, cleansing, even orgiastic. Lacan might say *jouissance*, and Freud *death drive*.

Lisbeth's rape by her new guardian in the film (and the book) is in many ways gratuitous. The same revenge scenario could have been played out without the rape/counter-rape by using only the videotape; but the profound horror of the rape scene, as well as the celebratory horror of the revenge rape, seem to function more as outrage-catharsis rides. I say that not because the rape was not possible, but because after the rape, in short order, Lisbeth quickly returns to her former psycho-sexual default position. She remains high-functioning, satisfyingly sexually active, and in control. She would have been more credible without the uber-violent rape in these guises, though some have argued that this was Lisbeth "refusing to be a victim." This notion of "refusing to be a victim" is a little troubling, in as much as it effaces the experience of victims who can't seem to just "refuse" a lot of things.

There *is* such a thing as victimization. There *is* such a thing as being a victim. And there are well-known reactions to being victimized by rape. Being a victim does *not* mean one "has no agency." Lord, the stupidity of popular culture's truisms! Being a victim means one has been wounded by an injustice.

Insomnia, anorexia, uncontrollable and unpredictable bouts of crying, hyper-vigilance, varying degrees of agoraphobia, inability to concentrate, fear and loathing associated with all sex, fear of being touched, fear of being alone, feeling helpless, substance abuse, nightmares, memory loss, and suicidal thoughts (and actions) are all well documented among rape survivors.[5] Lisbeth sleeps like a stone, continues to pound down junk food, never cries, engages fearlessly in all kinds of high-risk activity, has no trace of agoraphobia, concentrates like a laser, shags like a rabbit, retains her eidetic memory, and shows not a sign of a suicidal ideation. This is not only *not* credible, even in our super-heroine; it is a sanitizing affront to the experience of women (and men) who have been raped, which carries the message that, with enough strength of character (or vengeance) you can "get over it."

Whether it is Stieg Larsson, trying to shrive himself of guilt for not stopping or reporting a gang rape, or American screenwriter Steve Zaillian, trying to Tex-Mex the story into something acceptably American, the attempt by men to make this a story about men hating women, as a way of establishing their feminist *bona fides*, does not succeed except in a very "post-feminist" way. If rape, in addition to being eroticized violence, is about sexual objectification, male fantasies are all over the books and the film, and the male gaze in the American film-version is sovereign.

This is what I call the feminism-is-good-as-long-as-it-results-in-men-having-more-sex syndrome. Adrienne Rich, in writing about "compulsory heterosexuality," identified how men and women are indoctrinated with the belief that men have a *right* of access to female bodies.[6] Sexual access is an entitlement that requires even prostitution, if necessary, to satisfy it.

Carole Pateman gives us good reason to criticize the term *patriarchy* as the transhistorical rule of men, because after the merchant class's political revolutions against the European monarchies, what had been the absolute *rule of fathers* before became the contractual rule of what Freud called a "brother horde."[7] We might better call the rule of men *andrarchy*,

5. Capetown Trust Rape Crisis, "Rape Trauma Syndrome."

6. Rich, "Compulsory Heterosexuality," 11–48.

7. Pateman, *Sexual Contract*, 104.

which transitioned from one-father-rules (politically, the monarchy) to all-brothers-rule (republican democracy).

Pateman shows how psychoanalysts as well as political theorists have begun their accounts in story form, trying to trace existing dynamics of power back to some kind of "primal scene." The small-r republican form of governance, and the society of "liberty, equality, and fraternity" which it regulates, is based on a kind of patricide, the symbolic murder of the father (monarch) by the brothers (male citizens). Once the father is dead, however, there are so many brothers (the "brother horde").

"If brotherhood [fraternity] is to be maintained," says Pateman, "fraternal relations must be regulated."[8] This is the origin of the idea of the *social contract*, a contract between *brothers*. When the father (including the figurative father of the king) ruled, his absolute power had to extend over women (wives and daughters) as well, or it was not absolute. So in any primal scene, where we begin with the father, his fatherhood implies not only the right to rule, but the *sex-right* wherein his fatherhood originates in an act of coitus.

When the father is overthrown, the murderous brothers, in reestablishing order, have inherited not only political right, but *sex-right*. The control of and access to women by particular fathers-then-husbands is now the theoretical access of all men to all women. The *social contract* becomes the *sexual contract*, which was, in fact, enshrined in law by the marriage contract.

In order for one allegedly free woman to be protected from all men, she would have to *contractually* exchange obedience for protection with one man (a husband). This exchange is called *consensual*. She consented to making him her boss. The legal doctrine for a very long time for marriage was *couverture*, meaning a married woman's husband "covered" her in public dealings—he acted on her behalf, whereas his relationship with her was "hidden" (covert) from the law by the public-private separation. This doctrine was summed up as, "A man's home is his castle."

When feminists challenged this idea that men are entitled to access to women's bodies, it was met with an energetic backlash. Perhaps the slyest aspect of that backlash was the idea, promoted by men and uncritically adopted by some women, that "equality" between men and women means making women more like men. This includes celebrating female promiscuity matching male promiscuity and female violence matching male violence.

8. Ibid.

Sly, because in this scenario, the onus for change remains on . . . (surprise!) women; men continue to be as trifling as they always were, because they remain the standard to which women must aspire (or fail).

This is not denying that women's reclamation of their own sexual agency is a good thing in itself; but by staking all critical claims on this abstraction, we ignore the sexual reality of actual women's lives in a society where men's domination in every other sphere translates into far messier and less abstract power dynamics manifesting themselves in *all* sexual relations.

What happens to us when we come to associate sex with hostility?

8

Reluctant War and the Practice of Virtue: Katniss Everdeen

SUZANNE COLLINS, AUTHOR OF the *Hunger Games* novels and screenwriter for the films, was a military brat. She and her family were moved repeatedly. Collins's father, an Air Force officer, emphasized war history in the tutelage of his children.

Collins said during an interview once, "I believe he felt a great responsibility and urgency about educating his children about war. He would take us frequently to places like battlefields and war monuments. It would start back with whatever had precipitated the war and moved up through the battlefield you were standing in and through that and after that. It was a very comprehensive tour guide experience. So throughout our lives we basically heard about war."[1]

She became a writer for children's television; and before *Hunger Games* made her fabulously famous, she had already achieved a certain notoriety as the author of the *Underland Chronicles*, a youth fantasy series that also dealt with social turbulence and war. Susan Dominus, of the *New York Times*, said that Collins writes "war stories for kids."[2]

> Collins, a 48-year-old mother of two, spent much of her adult life writing for children's television, dreaming up plot lines for shows like "Wow! Wow! Wubbzy!" a Nick Jr. cartoon aimed at preschoolers. But in the "Hunger Games" trilogy, she revealed an outsize imagination for suffering and brutality. The books juxtapose the futuristic fantasy of a gleaming, high-tech capital and early-industrial life in the 12 half-starved districts it controls. In a ritual

1. Biography.com, "Suzanne Collins."
2. Dominus, "Suzanne Collins' war stories for kids."

> known as the Reaping, two adolescents from each of these oppressed districts are selected at random to participate in the Hunger Games, an annual televised match in which children battle one another and mutated beasts to the death, like Roman gladiators in a glitzy reality-TV contest. The trilogy's heroine, Katniss, 16 years old when the series begins, has the tough-girl angst of an S. E. Hinton teenager and is too focused on survival to spend much time on familiar Y.A. preoccupations like cliques and crushes. On the very first page, she stares at the family's pet cat, recalling, matter-of-factly, her aborted attempt to "drown him in a bucket." By the last book, she is leading a revolution.[3]

The *Hunger Games* film series, of all the films covered in this book, would be my first choice for my young granddaughters, if forced to choose one of these violent female leads. Nothing to do with the violence, my choice would be based on her eventual choice of a sexual partner, as un-feminist as that sounds at first blush, because for all the real women I know, one of the top two most significant choices they have made in their lives has been who shares their beds, the other being choice of profession (for those who actually *have* a choice). In more cases than I want to dwell on, especially but not exclusively in heterosexual relations, whatever initially attracts young women (and men) to potential partners is based on generally awful criteria if outcomes are any measure. For heterosexual young women, there is an enormous menu of really bad men out there from which to choose. And our culture teaches girls early how to desire most disastrously.[4]

Women, like men, are bombarded by cultural propaganda about what is and is not sexually desirable. In most films, including women action-hero films, the propaganda of sexual desire bends young women toward boys who are macho assholes or hopeless slackers. Men, by and large, develop this propaganda, and project their own self-serving fantasies into it.

In *Hunger Games*, the love triangle is between Katniss, the stereotypically macho Gale (who hunts with her), and the vulnerable Peeta (who Katniss rescues more than once). At the end of the series, Katniss does not end

3. Ibid.

4. This again, however, raises the issue of "compulsory heterosexuality," within which women's roles are still defined through an unequal complementarity. Katniss has finally retired as the kick-ass heroine and become a modest country mom, gazing idyllically between her baby and (admittedly and thankfully gentle) husband. On the other hand, if being a mother is antifeminist (it is not), then feminism would be closed to the majority of adult women. In Katniss's dystopian world, she is a sixteen- or seventeen-year-old bride, uncommon in some places, not in others.

up with Gale—whose macho approach to war leads him to sacrifice the innocent—but with Peeta, the boy who hates conflict, bakes bread, and wants to nurture children. This is a radical departure from film conventions; and if my heterosexual granddaughters are going to see a choice they may in some wise one day emulate, I'll go with Peeta every single time.[5]

There are several problems with this film—if only because it, like the rest, valorizes redemptive violence—but credit where credit is due. Collins hit the jackpot with this granddad on who is the more desirable partner. Blogger "Leopard," at *Crates and Ribbons* remarks, "Strength, honour and bravery are expressed in traditionally masculine ways when it comes to Gale . . . while the stereotypically feminine qualities of noble self-sacrifice in the name of love are found in Peeta." Odd, but I do believe that "self-sacrifice in the name of love" was also associated with an itinerant rabbi from Nazareth.

What is also peculiar to the *Hunger Games*, in the age of gender-as-expression, as opposed to gender-as-power-structure, is that in the *Hunger Games* series, ostentatious *expressions* of gender-bending—in clothing and mannerism, e.g.—are portrayed as a function of *privilege* among the Panem elite.[6] In a sense, Collins creates a world where gender (and even race) tension has been attenuated, with class as the most definitive form of power in a kind of post-apocalyptic, high-tech, tributary economy. Gender, as expression or power-structure, does not stand out from within the narrative, even though it is glaringly apparent to us, still living in a patriarchal world.[7]

Katniss begins her story as a surrogate "father" (read: protector/provider) in a household with a vulnerable little sister and a dependent, broken mother.[8] She protects and provides, even if her weapon of choice is a bow—which provides her with a stand-off lethality that compensates for less upper-body strength relative to biological males.[9]

5. Holmes, "Peeta, Her Movie Girlfriend," NPR's Linda Holmes tellingly referred to Peeta as "Katniss's girlfriend," in case anyone doubts my thesis that gender norms are preserved (and identifiable) in these films. Katniss is the honorary father. Peeta is an honorary girlfriend.

6. In *Hunger Games*, the gender transgressions are kind of clueless, over-aestheticized, and offensive spectatorship, a marker of ruling class moral decay.

7. The exception to this is that the government storm troopers all seem to be men.

8. The (weak) Mad Woman trope.

9. So much so that in one scene that defies all credibility she shoots down a fighter-bomber aircraft with an explosive arrow.

Let's look now at the ways that the *Hunger Games* series is similar to some of the films we have already discussed.

Like *Star Wars*, *Alien*, and *28 Days Later*, it is set in an imaginary future. Like *28 Days Later*, it is a dystopian future. Like *Star Wars*, the context is civil war. While *Tough Gynes*, in its specific selection of films, has shown a bias toward these future-fantasy scenarios, when *Indiewire* published its 2014 picks for top 25 "kick-ass" women in film, nine of them were fantasy genres, with an additional four as quasi-fantasies—films with very unlikely premises in "actual" circumstances, super-duper secret-agents and the like. Not surprising, because generally speaking, even in the male-dominated world of film, action films are predominated by precisely these kinds of fantasies. So while we might not be able to draw the conclusion that women who are "honorary men" in films require this departure from reality to give their characters credibility, we might at least suggest that placing women in these roles becomes more credible and acceptable in situations that are created apart from the more mundane and still-patriarchal reality that is most women's lives. When we are introduced to Katniss, she is clearly in an honorary male role relative to her mother and younger sister, and the visible gender norms of the hungry people of District 12 are pretty conventional.

Not to support, reinforce, or reassert conventional gender roles, there is an element of truth in this that we can see today, wherein those who most vociferously identify gender-convention transgressions, like cross-dressing and performative androgyny as cutting edge political resistance, are only those well-to-do or culturally-insulated people who can afford to get away with it. The single mom, hanging on by the skin of her teeth economically, does not go job hunting using "gender transgressive" displays and performances. That is not saying that gender transgression ought to be punished—quite the contrary. It is simply saying that certain kinds of transgressions are a function of privilege in a world where all conventions—gender and otherwise—are mutually policed in a cultural and economic matrix that is still dominated by rich people, with white and hetero-male predominating at the top of that heap. People who are vulnerable, at times even targets, are *not* trying to call attention to themselves. They are trying to blend in (camouflage?) in order to survive.

Like *Star Wars*, *Alien*, *28 Days Later*, and *Jane Got a Gun* (reviewed last in this series), *Hunger Games* is about a woman who is "forced to fight." Clarice Starling and Jordan O'Neil *chose* professions of arms; and Karen Crowder *chose* contract killing. What sets *Hunger Games* apart in this respect is that Katniss and the other fighters are not initially forced to face an enemy, but forced into gladiatorial combat *with one another* by a common oppressor.

This brings to mind that terrible paradox summarized by what novelist Walter Moseley called "ghetto pedagogy":

> Dad?
>
> Yes?
>
> Why do black men always kill each other?
>
> (Long pause.)
>
> Practicing.[10]

Violence, learned through oppression, is then seen as the means to escape it.

It also calls to mind C. L. R. James's dramatic history of the Haitian Revolution,[11] when various slave-rebel factions were forced to fight one another as allies of contending enemy colonial forces to gain the military proficiency they would need to eventually unite and defeat Napoleon's armed forces and win independence.

Katniss learns the art of warfare (and performative politics) first as a gladiator before leading her rebel forces against the Capitol. Of all the films we are examining in this book, this makes *Hunger Games* the most class conscious. But for all its class consciousness, which has been transferred from a capitalist economy into a dark fantasy of a tributary economy, and for all its gender-bending, the story conventions remain mired in a traditional patriarchal theme. Here is a test: if Katniss were a man, apart from the love triangle, would the story need to be substantially altered? Recognizing that the popularity of the series, written and in film, is based on the fact that Katniss is a (young white) woman, the conventions remain the same.

Class conscious, unlike *Star Wars*, this film mobilizes a gender-shifted republican/frontier masculinity in a kind of American Revolution myth

10. Mosley, *Black Betty*, epigraph.

11. James, *The Black Jacobins*.

redux, exactly like *Star Wars*. That's why *Hunger Games* maps as easily onto left-wing adventurist fantasies as onto right-wing adventurist fantasies. This trope is in the American cultural DNA. The small but plucky band of armed rebels, David-like, takes on the Goliath of a corrupt and unjust government/empire. Emboldened by the courageous and selfless acts of a heroic few, the oppressed population flocks to the banner of the brave hero(ine), rises up, and overthrows the tyrants.

Then we get chills and interpret the shivering tears elicited from us as sacred.

Other interesting parallels include Katniss/Jennifer Lawrence and Princess Leia/Carrie Fisher and the "fat" issue, who are both the (virginal) Hot Chick With a [Weapon]. Lawrence came under intense scrutiny from the movie industry as well as some critics for not being lean and ripped enough, ostensibly because she was from a poor district and ought to have been skinnier. Lawrence, like Fisher before they sent her to the "fat farm," is a fairly typical young woman, appears to have *almost* the *average* body fat for most young American women, which is between 24.8 and 29 percent. This is not only the average; it is better—healthwise—than the ten percent that modeling and acting agencies like—often maintained with cigarettes and stimulants, because low body fat for women can lead to a number of endocrine disorders . . . but, hey, health be damned, the standard is established and eroticized. We all have to make sacrifices.

And while the nabobs of the industry may not believe their own bullshit, young men remain entranced by weapon-exoticized women, as we mentioned earlier, and imagine themselves as the hyper-males who will win her over and gain sexual access: one reason that there was an online backlash by young men against Katniss's choice of Peeta. But what is even more interesting is how strong the backlash was among young women. *Teen Vogue* even weighed in on behalf of Gale.[12] Refusing the alpha male runs counter to the programming.[13]

Rolling Stone called Katniss "America's Kick-Ass Sweetheart." How would the *Hunger Games* series have played if the heroine had been (a) much older, (b) not "pretty," (c) not white, (d) 25 pounds heavier, etc.? The

12. Bonner, "Why Katniss Should Have Chosen Gale Over Peeta."

13. Lawrence was subjected to a hack of her personal computer to publish a series of nude selfies (which Lawrence described accurately as a sex crime), the virality of which demonstrated her perceived "hotness" among (overwhelmingly) male viewers.

film audience for the series was sixty-one percent female, which means that there were still substantial numbers of males[14] in the audience.[15]

Violence redeems the world in *Hunger Games*, and it does so through a series of *tempo tasks*. What is interesting and disappointing about *Hunger Games* is that in Gale we see how the instrumentality of violence and war are internalized—how the warrior comes to excuse violence, and how the violent revolution always results in a reliance on violence to secure the revolution's gains—yet Katniss has to use violence to prevent this outcome by killing the New Leader, Alma Coin, a cynically conniving, manipulative woman not unlike Senator Lillian DeHaven in *G.I. Jane*. The virtuous young woman has to kill off *another woman*—the Calculating Bitch—to resolve the final conflict.

Which brings us to the other women/girl characters in the film.

What we have, apart from Katniss herself, are (1) a Mad Woman (Katniss's mother), (2) helpless Angelic Females (Prim and Rue), (3) the Ditzy Broad (Effie Trinket), (4) the Calculating Bitch (Alma Coin and Johanna Mason), and a raft of Mean Girls (Cashmere, Foxface, Clove, Glimmer) who are fellow gladiators. Even female writers are drawn to many of the same gender conventions as their male predecessors;[16] but how would a sixteen-year-old reader or viewer recognize them were they not?

Katniss's honorary male-ness contrasts with her mother's more conventional character trope: a woman gone helplessly crazy with the loss of her man. In actual families where father-husbands die, mothers assume a greater degree of responsibility and control. Katniss defaults into a conventionally male role out of "necessity," in the same way women were hired to work in factory jobs during World War II when men joined the military (only to be pushed back out when the "boys" returned). The entire premise of the story begins with the necessity-driven substitution of a female for a male in a culture where (among the lower classes) gender conventions

14. Almost four out of ten.

15. Young, "Box office report." By comparison, the *Twilight Saga* drew 81 percent females, a film which—in accordance with standard patriarchal conventions—portrayed women as mindlessly love-starved for the affection of Bad Men. Again, recommending *Hunger Games* if there is a contest, though the issue of "compulsory heterosexuality" remains, for which some critics called the series a faux-feminist bait-and-switch.

Thaller, "Feminist Bait-and-Switch." For the record, on internet conversation boards populated by teens, Katniss Everdeen's feminist credentials were not the main topic; who she would choose as her boyfriend was. This speaks volumes.

16. Bodice-ripper romance novels are still very popular.

remain otherwise unperturbed. And when the war (necessity) is past, where do we find Katniss? Whispering to an infant and gazing at her husband. Substitution over! Honorary male reverts to normative female.

Kirstie Linstrom writes, "[M]any . . . critics analyze Katniss's ability to transcend stereotypical gender roles throughout the texts. Currently, these are the main scholarly conversations being held over *The Hunger Games*. While many of these critics have strong arguments, they all fail to address two alarming issues in the novels: the roles of the female characters and the influence the male characters have on them."[17]

When Katniss is drafted as a gladiator, her two main mentors are Haymitch, a man who teaches her fighting and instrumentality, and Effie, a woman whose sensibilities assist Katniss in navigating "reality" TV and the decadent fashions of the ruling caste. Apart from combat, with family as a prop for the demonstration of virtue, the main story revolves around the love triangle between Gale (manly storm) and Peeta (bread or a bird call).

At this juncture, we need to hit the pause button and take a little time with the above reference to "family as a prop for the demonstration of virtue."

When we obsessively decipher the masculinity and femininity of characters in doing gender critique, we are in danger of losing sight of what appeals to audiences who are unschooled in feminism and inattentive to gender: and that is *virtue*.

What makes Katniss Everdeen and Lisbeth Salander and Princess Leia attractive to audiences irrespective of gender is the same thing that has made most film protagonists attractive apart from sex appeal. They demonstrate, *within the moral context of the story and the shared worldview of the audience*, some form of ethical *integrity*.[18] Yes, Katniss Everdeen is "masculine" as a provider for her family and "feminine" in how selflessly she nurtures them; but for most audiences, if she were to do otherwise, she would be identified as lacking virtue (though not in those terms) and

17. Linstrom, "The Submissive, the Angel, and the Madwoman," 2.

18. *Virtue* in films is fairly easy to discover, and it's a very revealing hermeneutical gateway into precisely what people's (storied) moral contexts and (storied) worldviews are. In this way, cultural criticism offers us a refracted view of our most hidden and yet consequential social realities. Integrity is the quality of being authentic and honest, of trying to consistently demonstrate good will.

rejected. This is precisely why Katniss's character in the films, at least, is embraced by men/boys as well as women/girls who are viewing it without a gender-critical perspective. To explain this, we'll need a quick review of something called *virtue ethics*.

Virtue ethics is generally traced to Plato and Aristotle; and its late-medieval Aristotelian renaissance was facilitated by Moses Maimonides (Jewish); Thomas Aquinas (Christian); and Ibn Rushd, a.k.a. Averroes (Muslim).[19] Its modern advocacy is credited by some to Elizabeth Anscombe. Its most well-known present-day proponent is Alasdair MacIntyre (an "Aristotelian Thomist").

Ethics, as it is now studied, is generally presented as a set of quandaries. They are quandaries precisely because in our age, we have run into some problems with the development of rules that apply to everyone, everywhere, at all times; because in a pluralistic society "everyone" is not rooted in the same histories and traditions that give any organic coherence to the rules. And so we are left with an endless string of "ethical" dilemmas.

Do we donate the kidney to the sixty-five-year-old who was next in line; or do we bump up the thirty-year-old because she has longer to live anyway? Does the police character in your favorite cop show have a right to coerce a confession, even if it violates the law, when s/he knows the suspect is guilty; or is the primacy of the law and its equal application more important to preserve than one just outcome? Can the soldier on the recon kill one civilian who saw his unit on its way to a super-secret mission that could risk hundreds of lives if compromised? What these quandaries represent is the unresolvable tension between two predominant and contradictory approaches to ethical questions.

One approach says the rules imply a duty to strict rule-adherence even if it risks an occasional injustice. The other approach says "all's well that ends well," or "the ends justify the means." Rules and duties are secondary to outcomes. These two contradictory approaches, each with any number of justifying scenarios, are called "duty ethics" and "consequence ethics."[20] What Elizabeth Anscombe and Alasdair MacIntyre, among others, pointed out is that—in modern society—this contradiction never gets

19. Bender, "Lessons from the Three Wise Men." These three are credited with the philosophical renaissance of Aristotle, long set aside by Medieval Platonists. Averroes (1126–1198) had a strong following in the University of Paris, and that following was joined by Thomas Aquinas (1225–1274). Maimonides (1135–1204) was Averroes's contemporary, and was, likewise, a Spaniard. Aquinas studied them both.

20. Also called *deontological* ethics and *consequentialist* ethics.

resolved, because each assumes something similar: that there is no ultimate source of reference for right and wrong, which assumes one further thing: that in the absence of said authority, we need a *universal* standard by which to fairly judge ethical decisions.

The problem, says MacIntyre, is that people's situations are never universal, therefore no such universal standard is possible; and *this* problem is more acute the more diverse (or pluralized) a society is.

"I can only answer the question," writes MacIntyre, "of 'What am I to do?' if I can answer the prior question 'Of what story or stories do I find myself a part?'"[21]

Wait, what?

Stories again.

No rule can ever capture the complexity and unpredictability of life, and the story—truth, fiction, or parable—provides *context.* We instinctively know that stories require context, which is why we prefer, by and large, our moral lessons in the form of stories. All the films we are studying are stories. And what we are most interested in, with these stories, are the character's characters. It is not only that they find themselves in these situations that interests us, but specifically how they think and behave and relate to others in those situations. What virtues and vices do they demonstrate in their actions?[22]

Virtues and vices are character traits. *Virtue ethics* emphasizes the development of character[23] instead of advocating for either universal duty ethics or universal consequentialist ethics. The virtues are interconnected, rooted in practical activity, and discerned using *practical* reason. The virtue of courage, for example, cannot be fully ascertained, practiced, or evaluated apart from a specific (practical) act or without reference to another virtue, prudence. To act in a way that is fearlessly reckless is imprudent. Courage must also make reference to the virtue of justice. To be fearless in an unjust practice or act is not the "courage" we aim for to be a good person. Likewise, to refuse to take action, because of fear or timidity, to prevent an injustice, might seem prudent, but it is cowardly precisely because it is unjust. Connected.

21. MacIntyre, *After Virtue*, 216.

22. And how might that help me navigate my own life?

23. The commitment to do right combined with ability to discern the best course of action based on context. This is what we mean when we say, "So-and-so *has character.*"

When Katniss volunteers as a state gladiator in the place of her younger sister, we understand this as *courage*, not recklessness, because she is acting out of a care ethic, which is part of her character. When she gives Peeta another chance, after he has been brainwashed to attack her and her comrades, she is exercising the virtue of *charity*, expressed as forbearance and forgiveness, and motivated by love.

When we see Selena's ruthless consequentialism replaced by a selfless hesitation in her refusal to kill Jim when she doesn't know if he is infected or not, we all agree that she has achieved a greater degree of *virtue* in that selfless hesitation. When Lisbeth Salander takes on her job with Kalle Blomkvist, she is convinced not by the money, but by a desire to see *justice* for other women. When Clarice Starling rescues Catherine, her courage is not seen as reckless, but as *courage* in the service of a common good.

The audience wants to see a demonstration of virtue by a character, and this—more than anything else—will determine how strongly the audience will identify with that character. One time that character might show virtue by breaking the rules; another time, she might show virtue by risking bad consequences. The context of the story determines the virtuousness or viciousness of the action. Audiences crave demonstrations of virtue in their stories. And vice. We want someone to love and someone to hate. But we also want to be reminded that we, as human beings, have the capacity for good . . . for change and growth.

Here is where we have to return again to that analysis of gender as a system that divides power. As much as we like to see the bad guy get what's due in a police procedural, and to see it accomplished through the exercise of virtue, we also have to back up a bit and realize that this same film or program has *established a misleading notional context within which virtue is exercised.* The police consistently serve the common good, for example, or they serve the rich and poor equally, or "criminals" are all irredeemably evil (instead of broken, or crazy, or cornered by circumstance), or the police are part of a boundary between Us—the civilized—and Them—the barbarians.

Likewise, while there is much to recommend virtue ethics, and to recommend films that give us models (or anti-models) for virtuous action, our ideas about virtue are bound up in the context of the stories we have absorbed from our culture; and that culture is *patriarchal.* The virtue of courage, for example, is most often portrayed through violent combat; and courage in combat is a virtue associated with a kind of hegemonic masculinity that skips back in history from here to Westerns, to medieval knights, to King David.

Katniss is virtuous in exactly this way. It is a lot to think about.

Speaking of Westerns, let's take our final look at a recent Western that features a kick-ass female protagonist.

9

Conquest of the Frontier: Jane Hammond

Before we watch Natalie Portman as Jane Hammond in *Jane Got a Gun*, an American Western–genre film, we'll need to take a side excursion into the genre itself, because this genre of film (and television) provides several direct lines of sight on the intersection of American national masculinity with the American national myth.

First, some historical correction. The "history" of the American West, for a very long time, was, in fact, white American male mythology written as History. The reality was unimaginably different from the myth portrayed in films. Examples: settlers did not frequently clash with Native Americans, and settlers on the move seldom encountered "hostile Indians." Most of the conflict was between Native Americans and the government (via its cavalry). Gun violence was far lower than today, and firearms were strictly controlled. The actual pistols most often used were ball and cap affairs hardly accurate enough to shoot your own foot. Each shot made the gun so hot that the firer generally dropped it to nurse a blister. Cowboys were largely tutored by Mexican vaqueros (the origin of the term "buckaroo"), who were a third of all cowboys (with black men being one out of four—the Chinese, however, were imported to work as virtual slave labor). And cowboys worked, well, with cattle; not seeking out gunfights to save Beautiful Souls. There were 5,600 bank robberies in the US in 2010. During the post-Civil War Westward expansion, there were eight bank robberies. Cowboys didn't wear Stetsons, but most often bowlers, and sometimes hats that look like those of today's Amish.[1]

1. Nakamura and Wisniewski, "Five Ridiculous Myths."

Just as *Star Wars* originated as a Japanese film about Samurai (by a Japanese filmmaker influenced by Westerns), the American Western film traces its origins to medieval mythical romances featuring the Knight Errant.[2] The formula, which frequently includes a Damsel in Distress trope, is overlaid onto "dime novels"[3] of the westward moving US frontier. Originally portrayed by actors in scripts, the Western myth was promoted first in a carnival called Buffalo Bill's Wild West Show, then it jumped into moving pictures in 1894.[4] This was followed in the twentieth century by the increasingly popular Western pulp novels of Zane Grey, Louis L'Amour, Max Brand, and others.

With film reaching even non-readers, however, the mythology would eventually colonize the American social imaginary. The real United States had been troubled by the legacy of the Civil War, a split that was only partially healed when masses of white Southern and Northern soldiers went to the trenches together during World War I. The narrative that filled that space (the latter nineteenth century) was the idealized white narrative of westward expansion. In keeping with the knight errant theme, our heroes were almost always armed and riding a horse.[5]

Like all genres, the Western has been adapted for each succeeding zeitgeist. In fact is has become almost a canvas-genre, where various writers can paint what they like on it. From a fictionalized American pre-WWII progress myth, it was transformed into war propaganda, then social criticism, then anti-communist allegories for the Cold War, then antihero narratives for the sixties and seventies, and most recently into a handful of liberal/post-feminist stories.[6]

2. All genres that feature weaponized phalluses, whether guns, light sabers, or swords and lances.

3. Fictionalized accounts of actual people: Billy the Kid, Wyatt Earp, Jesse James, et al., many of them petty criminals (including the law enforcement officers) more interested in inflating their reputations than anything else.

4. Yes, American popular culture did assimilate its main ideas about a period of history based on the racist productions of a carnival barker. Now one is the President. William "Buffalo Bill" Cody (1846–1917) was himself a great admirer of William Sherman, who called for outright Indian extermination, and of George Custer, whom he saw as a white martyr. Cody's show, usually billed alongside military tournaments, reenacted "battles" between white men and Indians that emphasized Indian savagery and white nobility.

5. In the old TV Western, *Have Gun Will Travel*, the theme song calls its hero "a knight without armor in a savage land."

6. Like *The Quick and the Dead*, *The Ballad of Little Jo*, *Bad Girls*, *Gang of Roses*, and *The Missing*.

Film Westerns first won their popularity during the Great Depression, when mass unemployment created a crisis of masculinity among American white men.[7]

> In the United States, Hollywood was mobilized as a palliative. Chirpy movies with happy endings became a major film entrée. Westerns were most popular with men and boys. The Western hearkened to American mythical frontier masculinity, portrayed by "virile" men—heroic, autonomous characters who dominated women, land, animals, and savages, a story of mastery and control as the antidote to the vagaries of the Great Depression.
>
> "The hero's triumph over the wild things dramatizes the mastery of the patriarchy," writes Margery Hourihan. Virility breaks down the resistance of all things passive—and we see in many films, as well as in bodice-ripper literature, how the female lead nearly swoons before the masculine mojo of the leading man.[8]

When the war came, of course, Westerns were displaced by war films; but when the war ended, Westerns became the Cold War favorite in the US.[9] In 1947, major American filmmakers did fourteen Western movies. In 1948, they did thirty-one. By 1956, they were up to forty-six a year. From then until the early seventies, Westerns were consistently the most popular film genre in the US, netting a third of all American moviegoers.[10]

7. Men, who in the postwar era were encouraged to see themselves as providers for their families, were either cast adrift on the job market or forced into working conditions they would not have heretofore accepted. Unemployed men found their wives less subject to them, especially when the wives were finding spot work unavailable to men. Children listened more to their mothers than their fathers. Drunkenness was accompanied far more frequently by men physically attacking their wives; and for many men the "pansy" became a target for their violent insecurities. Active *widespread* homophobic violence came to the fore for the first time in the United States during the Great Depression.

8. Goff, *Borderline*, 316.

9. Westerns supported the peculiar military adventure in Korea in as much as they inscribed racialized and militarized boundaries between civilization and threat. The popular Marine Colonel Lewis "Chesty" Puller—a good friend of Western film director John Ford (*Fort Apache*, *Rio Grande*, et al.)—gave a speech to his troops in Korea, exhorting them to write to their families about getting "harder" for America: "Tell 'em there's no secret weapon for our country but to get hard, to get in there and fight. I want you to make 'em understand. Our country won't go on forever, if we stay soft as we are now. There won't be an America—because some foreign soldiers will invade us and take our women and breed a hardier race."

10. Goff, *Borderline*, 367.

> The postwar Western movie had several archetypical storylines: the town-tamer, the cavalry and the Indians, the revised outlaw, the gunfighter, the High Noon showdown, and the good man with a gun. The Western genre gave each of these narratives a wide "mythic space" in which to tell these differing stories. Cold War Westerns all had some defining borderline, whether it was a river, a fort's palisade, a street, a fence, or the (fragile) boundary between civilization and wilderness, or savagery. A hero or protagonist had to cross those borderlines and by transgressing them "reveal the meaning of the frontier line" as he entered the dark side to protect the good side. Sometimes, after we were schooled in the psychoanalytic wolf-man, as the protagonist dealt with the "darkness" across the border, he also dealt with the darkness within himself. It is always a he. In the Western, the audience was to understand the boundary that separates their past from the viewing present, and therein they understood this to be a tale of progress. Last but certainly not least, there was a resolution, a "regeneration" accomplished by male violence . . .
>
> "A cowboy will not submit tamely to an insult," said Theodore Roosevelt,[11] "and is ever ready to avenge his own wrongs; nor has he an overwrought fear of shedding blood. He possesses, in fact, few of the emasculated, milk-and-water moralities admired by the pseudo-philanthropists; but he does possess, to a very high degree, the stern, manly qualities that are invaluable to a nation."
>
> Women in the Cold War Western were portrayed as either markers of civilization and domesticity or threats to manhood—sometimes both at the same time. "While the essential qualities of womanhood that tie women to domesticity are nostalgically honored in Westerns," writes Edward Buscombe, "femininity as a social force is represented as a threat to masculine independence and as the negative against which individual masculinities are tested."[12]

In breaking with the Cold War motifs during the seventies, Westerns kept a good deal of the machismo, but dropped the ethical artifices, as they did in the "Spaghetti Westerns," or they tried to become edgier (with sex especially, Hollywood's go-to for increasing market share) with more "modern" sensibilities (usually portrayed by revising mythical hair and clothing fashions, or thumbing their noses at "virtue"). *McCabe and Mrs. Miller* comes to mind. Recent attempts at "Western realism," like the *Deadwood*

11. Roosevelt was a big booster of the frontier masculinity myths, a man obsessed with proving his own masculinity, and a strong supporter of US Indian removal policies as well as aggressive American imperial expansion.

12. Goff, *Borderline*, 368–69.

series, have constructed a detail-fiction around broad historical "facts," and to make sure we know they are "realistic," they have plenty of nudity, sex, and bad language, ensuring the insertion of the term "cocksucker" into every other sentence of the script for almost every character in the series, even non-English speakers![13]

Given all the shape-shifting of the genre, let's move in now and take a closer look at *Jane Got a Gun*[14] and its titular character, Jane Hammond, played by Natalie Portman. Directed by Gavin O'Connor, whose films include macho gun-and-sports fare like *The Accountant*, *Warrior*, *Pride and Glory*, and *Miracle*, *Jane Got a Gun* features a protagonist who is "hot," and therefore contested for by three men, a former boyfriend, her current dying husband, and a vicious pimp. Jane can tell sweet bedtime stories to a child and knead bread, then shoot a man to death, without a ripple of change in her general affect, and she is up against a gang of violent Olde West™ pimps who want to kill her kind but only marginally desirable husband. The pimps want to traffic her and her young daughter. No, Jane is not, like Ellen Ripley, a man's part in the script that gets changed by altering pronouns. She is, nonetheless, a "postfeminist" honorary male . . . when she needs to be . . . who can still "have it all": good looks, a nuclear family, a "bad boy" hunky-man, and if necessary, the willingness and ability to blow some raping, murdering bastard's brains out.

Our frontier woman is white, and she has subtly and skillfully applied makeup, well-plucked brows, perfect teeth (great dentists back in the day), and neither scar nor blemish nor callused hands. Her husband ("Bill Hammond," played by Noah Emmerich) returns from somewhere afar, across

13. There is plenty of what some call gender-bending (Calamity Jane, e.g.), and some even call the series a critique of masculinity. I am skeptical of this claim, and only note that the series was wildly popular among males, young and middle-aged, because it (again!) presented a world where men could prove themselves openly and unapologetically through violence and misogyny, albeit without the encumbrances of today's "political correctness." In this way, it reminds me of extreme sports, where the virtue of courage is separated from any meaningful application that would make it virtuous. The expression of violent masculinity is unencumbered in *Deadwood* by the traditional Western's emphasis on guarding the border between civilization and barbarism, or protecting good women from bad men and savages. Instead, we get Hobbes on the frontier.

14. A peculiar aside here about provenance: *Jane Got a Gun* is a semantic takeoff on *Janie Got a Gun*, an Aerosmith tune, which was in turn cribbed from the Dalton Trumbo antiwar novel, *Johnny Got His Gun*. So in this declension, the gun goes from an object of ironic ridicule to critique men's violence, to an abused child's means of redemptive violence against a male, to redemptive violence in the form of a weaponized phallus for the ascension of a woman into honorary male-hood (also through redemptive violence).

the great empty Western landscape, to her smiling welcome, then falls off his horse just outside their cabin. After being cruelly wounded by the evil gang of pimps and thieves, the plosively alliterated "Bishop Boys," he fortuitously manages to stay astride of his mount until just arriving home. The Falling Off Your Horse in Front of the House trope.[15]

Jane goes into action. She somehow drags a 220-pound man into the house and onto the bed, where she expertly removes his bullets and cauterizes his wounds with gunpowder removed from a bullet. Once she has stabilized her patient, she (expertly again) loads her gun, puts on her Stetson and long black coat, and after a good deal of cloyingly clichéd dialogue wherein she discovers the Bishop Boys are coming for her husband, she mounts her steed, drops her child off with a friend (leaving her unencumbered for battle), and gallops away to seek the aid of Dan Frost (played by Joel Edgerton), a gunfighter.[16]

When she arrives at Frost's cabin, finding him in a dissipated state (no cliché *here*), surrounded by strewn empty bottles, we have a reveal scene. She and Frost have a sexual history—which will be further elucidated with a schmaltzy string of flashbacks. He refuses, and the dramatic tension is established. Find a doctor, he tells Jane. Her reply is classic redemptive violence: "I don't need a doctor. I need a gunslinger."

There's killin' t' be done.

Enter John Bishop in the flesh, head villain of the Bishop Boys, played by a prosthetically-disguised and soul-patched Ewan McGregor (for the Weirdest Casting of the Decade award), torturing a man to find the whereabouts of his obsessive object of revenge, Bill Hammond, who had secreted fair Jane away from the Bishop Boys some years earlier. John Bishop is a man who can hold a poisonous grudge.

Switching back, Jane arrives in Hardbitten Stereotypical Westerntown, where she goes to the General Store and purchases guns, ammunition, and dynamite (because everyone knows how to use dynamite). Here we see the wanted poster: John Bishop, Reward: Dead or Alive. $5,000. $5,000 in that era and place would be around a billion dollars now, so our chief antagonist must be One Bad Hombre.

15. Kidding.

16. Horses in Westerns always gallop, often for hundreds of miles, which suggests a now-extinct breed, because horses who actually gallop that long and often are on the short list for vulture lunch.

Flashback: Missouri, early days of the Civil War. People are actually wearing bowler hats, which suggests that the bowler-to-Stetson transformation must have been enforced once men crossed certain state or territorial boundaries. Plenty of trees meant you wore the bowler. Sand, sagebrush, and rocks? Wear the Stetson.

Jane and her paramour Frost are young people in love. In one particularly awful scene as Frost is preparing to enlist and do his duty, he and Jane ride a hot air balloon for some high altitude smooching, which will lead to the farewell-for-war encounter that leaves Jane "with child."

The separation for the war then hardens Frost as a soldier and prisoner, forging his future as a gunslinger.

Bishop, in this flashback, is the cheroot-sucking menace heading up a wagon train aimed West (to open a chain of whorehouses), with his gang (some of whom are facially tattooed and greasy-looking to make them very extremely sinister).

Flash forward to Hardbitten Stereotypical Westerntown again. Jane is spotted by one of the Bishop Boys, a repulsively seedy man-weasel who corners Jane in a back alley and taunts her by jacking off his gun (oh, but they're not phallic symbols). This rape threat causes Frost, reluctant gunslinger and father of her (now lost) child, to materialize just in the nick of time. Frost and the outlaw aim their guns at each other in what has been called the Mexican Standoff trope.[17] While they are exchanging threats, Jane—laying on the ground—shoots the outlaw in the head for our first good dose of Peckinpah-style enhanced splatter. I guess Jane has the more potent penis after all.

Once the first act is in, *Jane Got a Gun* is slowly developed as a David-Goliath siege drama, like the Alamo or Masada, except the Alamo and Masada were real, and those Davids all died, and their enemies triumphed in battle. By *siege drama*, I mean when the action is structured by someone trying to survive while being surrounded by a much larger hostile force. *The Two Towers*, anyone? Wikipedia lists 58 films as "siege films." Western siege

17. In addition to being a racist term, the trope itself is incredibly stupid, and therefore used again and again by filmmakers. The thing about "gunfighting" is that once aimed, a firearm is only a finger press (millisecond) away from discharging. This means the time between decision to shoot and the action is a millisecond, faster than anyone can possibly respond to it. In reality, once two people commit to gunplay, survival is based on firing with absolutely no hesitation. Two people do not threaten each other this way long enough to have conversations.

dramas include seven films about the Alamo alone,[18] as well as *Rio Bravo, El Dorado, Last of the Comanches,* and *The Magnificent Seven.* The moral lines in siege dramas are clear. There is one side you root for, and another you root against. The dramatic tension is developed by the incommensurate power between the more formidable (at first glance) Bad Guys and the comparatively weak (at first glance) Good Guys. We in the audience are leaning forward in our seats, breathless to know how they can possibly get out of this. With the *Alamo* movies, of course, since history does still hold some extremely tenuous sway over the narrative, the defenders shall all go down to Sheol. RIP. Shit happens. But in the less restricted and more commercially optimistic films, like *Jane Got a Gun,* if you walk out of the theater feeling like someone just shot your dog, you won't exactly be a great ambassador to others about the film. Word of mouth is a killer in films. We kind of know in advance that the Good Guys will somehow prevail. But we're still holding our breath to know *how.* If that makes little sense, then we can add some high-fructose special effects to distract and entertain you.

Preparing for The Siege, we have the march-musicky Prepare For Battle Interval, to get that quivering frisson of bloodlust worming through our scalps. Cue the music. Jane and Frost, under Frost's supervision as a former Civil War soldier, begin to prepare the defenses of the house as the Bishop Boys, the armies of Mordor writ small, approach like a distant storm. The work of untold female labor hours, the canned food in the cellar, is dumped out to convert the feminine canning jars into masculine kerosene bombs.[19] Frost is digging a trenchline around the house, and seeding it with the kerosene jars and gunpowder. Obviously he has some secret military trickery up his sleeve, that clever devil! Jane is getting guns ready and looking after the medical necessities for her half-conscious, shot-up husband.

When one member of the gang shows up for a reconnaissance, Frost shoots him, then tortures him, then shoots him again to dispatch him. This

18. Always presented as a plucky band of civilized settlers fighting off hordes of bad Mexicans; when in fact the reason for the Texas Rebellion was that white American settlers wanted to own slaves, and slavery was outlawed in Mexico.

19. Just by the by, speaking as one who used explosives for some time, kerosene would make a dud bomb, because though it ignites quickly, it does not explode, even under pressure, but for a very short distance, leaving behind a thin fire that can easily be extinguished. Kerosene, and even gasoline, will be "blown out" with the addition of high explosives, unless there is an added incendiary to re-ignite the fuel. In the movies, all explosions have fireballs—a trick accomplished with liberal supplies of gasoline mixed with incendiaries (steel wool works, as does thermite). In reality, high explosives without added incendiaries are relatively free of visible flame.

is the *tempo task*, which justifies torture, so long as it is inflicted on someone who the audience has already been taught to revile. Torture always works best in films if we are given an appetizer of disgust—the reason bad guys are frequently portrayed as unhygienic. At least they were white guys, instead of Indians; but then in this film about the Olde West™, we find a land utterly unpopulated by any indigenous people. Jane doesn't like the Indian(less) land she is on; she wants Indian(less) land in California. Westward, our civilization from sea to shining sea.

To build Hollywood, civilization's highest achievement.

There is a shootout, of course, during which it looks like the end for our heroes; but they prevail through trickery, with only the wounded husband dying, leaving Jane free to more or less virtuously reestablish her love affair with Frost. Oddly, as in many films, though there are storms of gunfire, and dead people everywhere, the horses manage to get away unscathed.[20]

They have Bishop in hand now, whereupon Jane gives her best Dirty Harry meets Mama Bear Trope to discover the whereabouts of her daughter (who she thought was dead, but turns out to be alive). The Gun becomes the mediating character: Do I have a bullet left, or not? Do you feel lucky, punk? They are then reunited with her daughter—which makes them a good, heteronormative nuclear family, who can now collect the fortune in reward money (a Deuteronomical twist) and fulfill the dream of going to California.

Is Jane an honorary male? Well, yes, but only temporarily—like Selena in *28 Days Later*—who can now put her gun in the closet and get about the business of baking bread for Frost and her daughter . . . in mythical California, the final point in "the conquest of the frontier."

Now, if you are doing a group study and have the time and inclination, together choose a tenth film featuring a violent female lead. Watch it, and apply any of the ideas, perspectives, or spinoff topics you have discussed before, or find a different critical perspective to apply. All good fun.

20. During my work as a technical advisor on a film, there was likewise a battle scene in which animals miraculously survived. When I asked why, there were two main reasons: first, it is an expensive and time-consuming process to anesthetize animals or make good models; second, audiences become more outraged at dead animals than they do human beings.

10

The F-word

Every binary split creates a temptation to merely reverse its terms, to elevate what has been devalued and denigrate what has been overvalued. To avoid the tendency toward reversal is not easy—especially given the existing division in which the female is culturally defined as that which is not male. In order to challenge the sexual split which permeates our psychic, cultural, and social life, it is necessary to criticize not only the idealization of the masculine side, but also the reactive valorization of femininity.

—Jessica Benjamin[1]

FILM OR FEMINISM? WELL, we've done nine films, so let's go back and revisit feminism.

What is it?

Liberal feminism claims feminism as a movement to allow individual women to do as they like. This has the same problem as liberalism generally has with regard to other movements for sociopolitical emancipation: it refuses to recognize the organized nature of oppression, and thereby limits the scope of social movements, which risks depoliticizing some of those who are targeted by systemic oppression. It is a *me*-feminism that mitigates against solidarity, making it the "safer" form of feminism. Following Jesus is incompatible with *me*-feminism, but not with the *feminist* aspect. Incompatible with the *me*. Jesus is the absolute opposite of Me First anything. Our argument ought to be with Me, not with Feminists.

Feminism and womanism[2] are simultaneously a movement, a collection of theories, a constellation of practices, and several forms of criti-

1. Benjamin, *Bonds of Love*, 8.
2. Which I abbreviate as "feminism," without any valuation except general familiary.

cal discourse. These are all related to one another around a *project*. That project aims at the elimination of injustices in the social relations between men-as-a-class vis-à-vis women and women-as-a-class vis-à-vis men, and the injustices to sexual minorities rationalized within the ideology of compulsory heterosexuality.

This project begins with the recognition that men-as-men benefit from existing social relations in ways that come at the expense of women-as-women, and through the policing of this systemic power, via gender norms, and at the expense also of sexual minorities.[3] This social arrangement of male-class dominance and privilege, abstracted across time and cultures, is what we call patriarchy (the rule of fathers) and/or andrarchy (the rule of men). I'll just call it patriarchy, because it is a well-recognized term now for male rule.

Men's domination of, exclusion of, and contempt for women has taken on many forms, in many time and places. This domination, exclusion, and hatred of women have, in themselves, been remarkably transhistorical and transcultural. Gendered power is tangled up with all other power asymmetries, like race, nationality, kinship, and class. What makes this gendered aspect of power particularly stubborn is twofold: first, gender ideology is indoctrinated almost from birth, and so is experienced almost as natural, or as common sense; second, in these other forms of power asymmetry, the oppressor is not *generally* connected to the oppressed in many intimate relations.

> Whereas the power relations between men and women are similar to those between dominated and subordinated classes and ethnic groups, the day to day context in which these power relations are played out is quite different. It is not a cultural norm for each working class individual to be paired up for life with a member of the middle class or for every black person to be so paired up for life with a white person. However, our traditional gender ideology dictates just this kind of relationship between men and women.[4]

So a mother, who suffers injustice as a woman, may be raising a son, who will benefit from those same unjust relations. Even for a *feminist* mother who is raising sons, her worldview as a feminist will be confronted and resisted day in and day out, by schools, advertising, music, film, television,

3. Gender norms, like masculinity and femininity, are embedded in the broader structural and ideological reality of "compulsory heterosexuality."

4. Eckert, "The Whole Woman," 253–54.

and peer pressure, all of which participate in a sustained, incessant, and better accepted and *contrary* world-view. And this cultural indoctrination is allowed nearly unfettered access to the young with little to no moral concern for or moral awareness of the messages or the methods. Gender, as an ideology in support of patriarchy, even manages to infiltrate our sexuality—our very bodies—training us in what is and what is not sexually desirable. Many men really *do* get off on women's sexual humiliation. Many women really are attracted to "dangerous" men. Doesn't often end well.

Gender—again, meaning a division of social power between men and women that also adversely affects sexual minorities—is substantially sustained by its ideological appearance as natural, or common sense. Film *criticism*, as an influential form of critical discourse, can expose the ways in which film characters, plots, themes, and conventions serve to reinforce the patriarchal assumptions into which all of us, regardless of how our *bodies* were "sexed" at birth, are indoctrinated.

> From a feminist perspective, the prevailing conception of gender is understood as an ideological structure that divides people into two classes, men and women, based on a hierarchical relation of domination and subordination, respectively. Based upon sexual difference, the gender structure imposes a social dichotomy of labour and human traits on women and men, the substance of which varies according to time and place . . . Although as individuals people may deviate from the archetypes of masculinity and femininity pertinent to a community, this nonetheless occurs against the ideological structure of gender that privileges men as a social group, giving them . . . a 'patriarchal dividend', in terms of access to symbolic, social, political, and economic capital.[5]

Being a woman is not the same as being feminist, but being feminist (or a supporter) presupposes—at a bare minimum—trying to assume the standpoint of women, not simply as individuals, but as a class of people who are subject to a provisionally common standpoint (marked as women) in the face of a provisionally common problem: men, telling them who they are and what they can and cannot do. Feminism is a political movement that defines itself as *for* women-as-a-class and *against* patriarchal domination. Many women are not feminists. Many women have established themselves *comparatively* comfortably within a patriarchal society, as well as internalized the ideas and values of patriarchy. And many people simply scratch by,

5. Lazar, "Feminist Critical Discourse Analysis," 146.

without access to the experience, time, and resources for informed participation in political matters. Feminists, in addition to opposing male rule, try to raise the consciousness of other women to see themselves as part of the class-of-women, as opposed to simply individual women.

Feminism, when it was explicit in its call for solidarity among women as an historically-constructed class, had substantial victories within the larger framework of democratization, victories on a par with the struggle for racial equality or the eight-hour workday. Sexual harassment is now a crime in many places, and that was a campaign mounted by feminists. Marital rape was not even recognized as a crime; and it is now illegal in every US state. Feminists did that. Women are forty-six percent of medical students in the US and fifty-one percent of law students. This is a good thing. Feminism added a new and—I would argue, the deepest—dimension to the struggle for authentic popular democracy; but it has been stalled by both backlash and cooptation, about which we will say more further down.

Feminism/feminists are *not* "against men," though there is quite simply no way to articulate feminism's concerns without attending to men-as-a-dominant-class, which means saying things that may discomfit most men. An African-American feminist/womanist may be simultaneously critical of African-American patriarchy and still stand united with the same African American men in opposition to white supremacy. Many, many feminists are the mothers of males; and many are married to males; and many have healthy, respectful relations with particular males in and out of their families.

More men need to be involved in the feminist project, as "allies" to be sure,[6] but most urgently for us to begin addressing in ourselves and our male peers, in more than rhetorical ways, the ways in which we are most complicit with these injustices. Feminists will continue to resist their own oppression and that of other women and sexual minorities who are excluded and despised based on patriarchal gender norms; and the best way men can resist the injustices of gendered power is by learning how to *quit doing things that perpetuate it or make it worse.* "*Primum non nocere.*"[7]

The first step, for men, in doing what is necessary to correct gendered injustices, is to get our heads around the difference between a critique of

6. A popular (and ever more reified) term for which various people would like to list the criteria: *ally*. In a sense, the term is more applicable to people who are active in political struggles, where the world gets divided into allies and enemies.

7. "First, do no harm." A medical principle.

men-as-a-class and a personal attack. Someone saying you enjoy certain privileges as a male is not a personal attack. It is a statement of fact that does not impugn your moral character. Our defensiveness on this account is twofold: it can be based on an unrecognized discomfort we have with losing our own privilege or with the ways in which feminist analysis might point to our own complicity in a system of power that we didn't recognize because we were its beneficiaries; and it can be partly our ahistorical inability to conceive of anything except "individuals." It's time for us to show up and grow up. Especially Christian men, because we are called to justice and sacrificial service, and we are called to stand nonviolently *against* domination. Patriarchy is domination; it is *not* love.

Returning, then, to feminism itself, there are several schools of feminism, and some of them stand in contradiction to one another on particular issues. We've roundly criticized liberal feminism for its tendency to exclusively "gender" all questions of oppression without attention to intersecting forms of social domination, like racial, national, and economic oppression.[8]

Likewise, our critical engagement with several films questions the now popular notion (originating in the Academy and being taken up by the well-privileged "artistic" community that makes most films) that "transgressing" gender norms, for example, by flipping the scripts between men and women, is somehow "disrupting" gender as a system that divides power between men and women, by muddying the popular understandings of *masculine* and *feminine*. I believe theatrical transgressions have a time and place in politics; I am simply saying that (1) it is not a panacea, and (2) it is a marker of privilege. In practice, however, these symbolic "disruptions" that leave masculinity and femininity de-historicized and decontextualized have had precious little political effect on the lives of most women. Part of the reason is that this "performance" of gender—not as power structure, but as a menu of mix-and-match gender artifacts—is neither available to the vast majority of women still constrained by the social structures that the privileged have managed to escape, nor does this mix-and-match "transgressive" approach deal with the *content* of these various gender conventions. Does a man dressing as a hyper-fem woman really undermine femininity constructed

8. This accusation has been leveled against "second wave" feminism, which is something of a red herring; because "second wave" encompasses several and often opposed threads of feminist inquiry. The more radical feminists of the so-called "second wave" were clear and explicit about these intersections, and several of the key "second wave" feminists were, in fact, women of color. The "wave" taxonomy for feminism is a faulty signifier.

as helpless, decorated, self-objectification? Does a white woman with a gun, killing Arabs, really undermine an imperial masculinity constructed as conquest of brown colonial others?

> [T]hese gender crossings index (and perpetuate) the underlying dualism of the gender structure—the behaviour of the masculine woman and the feminine man gets read against the expected behavioural norm of the "other".[9]

And so these so-called transgressions, in addition to reinforcing class differences through a display of transgressive *privilege*, can serve to reinforce notions of complementarity and "compulsory heterosexuality," the very origins of masculinity and femininity, which are the very ideological bases of patriarchal control. The basic ideological power structure that relates *objectification* to *domination* remains untouched, because we evade highlighting what is *wrong* with objectification and domination. I don't believe it is an accident that this brand of transgressive "resistance" is inherently depoliticizing, and that this perspective became an academic dogma . . . then a mass cultural production. This is part of a sly backlash against feminism, which has not surprisingly been called "post-feminism," and which has endeavored to erase "woman" as a category (and therefore as a political identity).[10]

Some will say that I am confusing postmodern feminism with post-feminism; and they are different, if only because there are now multiple "schools" of postmodern feminism. But the self-fragmentation, interpreted by postmodernists as human nature (a putting on of theatrical masks concealing a will to power), and celebrated by post-feminists (as

9. Lazar, "Feminist Critical Discourse Analysis," 148.

10. Gill, "Post-feminist media culture." The term *post-feminism*, like feminism and postmodernism, has emerged unscathed from the Academy into the streets of mass-media culture. There is little rigor in the application of the term, but it is suggestive in very sly ways. Rosalind Gill tried to correct this cloudiness by describing *post-feminism* first as a sensibility. This works here, because film fiction depends far more heavily on our least critical and most familiar sensibilities than it does on analytic/synthetic thought that might destabilize those sensibilities. Gill says that the *sensibility* of post-feminism, which she points out entangles feminist and anti-feminist characteristics, includes the following: (1) "the notion that femininity is a bodily property": (2) "the shift from objectification to subjectification"; (3) "the emphasis on self-surveillance, monitoring, and discipline"; (4) "a focus on individualism, choice, and empowerment"; (5) "the dominance of a makeover paradigm"; (6) "a resurgence in ideas of natural sexual difference"; (7) "a marked sexualization of culture"; (8) and "an emphasis on consumerism and commodification of difference."

freedom, even from solidarity with other women), is the reflection, in a de-traditionalized epoch (modernity), of *Homo optionis* (the consumer) and *Homo economicus* (the uprooted individual) progressively overthrowing those pre-capitalist, premodern stories, practices, and kinships around which identity was formed. Popular interpretations of postmodern feminism have this in common with post-feminism. Both begin with the myth of uprooted, decontextualized personhood, one as an academic excursion, and another as a sales pitch.

> Postmodernist understandings of "gender as performance" . . . have been notably problematic for some feminists, who rightly point out that there is a tendency to locate everything in discourse and overlook experiential and material aspects of identity and power relations. That is, instead of viewing discourse as one element of social practices, the inclination has been to view discourse as wholly constitutive of the social. Also problematic from a critical feminist perspective is the celebration of individual freedoms to perform transgressive acts like cross-dressing or cross-talking, which are not tantamount to a radical subversion of the gender structures; indeed, as I mentioned, such acts may unwittingly help reinforce those very structures.[11]

We emphasized earlier that stating all women are not feminists does not denigrate women who aren't. I hope instead that I have highlighted some of the ways in which hegemonic ideologies—gendered and not—are incorporated into the worldviews of us all. That is what *hegemonic* means.[12]

Film, in particular, an industry long dominated by rich white men, is unlikely to be the medium for a great deal of serious counter-cultural resistance, though it retains tremendous potential. In fact, film tends to magnify the cultural trends that are seen as the trendiest, "sexiest," and most "cutting edge" (read: commodifiable) among the social groups of the filmmakers themselves. If strong women characters are seen as trendy and/or profitable, Hollywood and its ilk will produce strong women characters; but they will then drain them, by design or default, of their most fundamentally subversive and authentically counter-cultural qualities, beginning with ensuring that female leads—no matter how strong—remain fuckable.

Only with the erasure of women as political subjects can postfeminism get away with suggesting that, because some women have become

11. Lazar, "Feminist Critical Discourse Analysis," 150–51.

12. When a ruling consensus "feels like" common sense.

successful in the competitive rat race that was formerly men's, we can put all that second-wavy political stuff behind us now.

The dominant ideology of late or postmodernity is still liberal *individualism*, with an emphasis on purchased "lifestyles." Liberalism bucks against any form of ethical restraint and effectively extinguishes the bases for collective action (especially political action), except worship of the twin idols of appetite and accomplishment.

"The process of turning feminism into sign values," says Robert Goldman, "fetishizes feminism into an iconography of things. When advertisers [and filmmakers] appropriate feminism, they cook it to distill out a residue—an object: a look, a style."[13]

Whether they are being trendy, capitalizing on an upsurge in popularity, adjusting their self-presentation, or trying to smuggle the hegemonic ideology back into a mode of resistance (to neutralize it?), the individual, purely-symbolic "strong woman" character is not only not always representative of a feminist project, she may be deployed as a what firefighters call a "backfire," or a controlled burn to destroy the fuel that could facilitate the spread of a wild fire.

One problem with the term "equality," as opposed to emancipation, is that it easily translates into *equality* meaning women becoming *like men*. Not only like men, but like powerful, heteronormative, "well-adjusted," white men. This is even true, for example, in film portrayals of racial minorities or gay characters or people with handicaps, who, before they can be acceptable, are shown to be in all other respects exactly like that hygenic, heteronormative, "well-adjusted," white man. Because the ostensibly neutral, universal norm into which we must all be assimilated is neither neutral nor universal. You can join the club, but only as an honorary white man doing those things that our iconic white man has done all along—he formed the whole world with his image, his story, his background music.

Work obediently. When the time comes, redeem the world with some organized violence.

We can have a black body and/or a woman's body, and even a disabled body, for example, but the action, the principle, the powerfully affective story of *redemptive violence* remains untouched; and the *actual* character of violence, that is still disproportionately concentrated against those same kinds of bodies to preserve existing structures of power, stays behind the curtain.

13. Goldman, *Reading Ads Socially*, 131.

The old warlike, colonial boundaries "between (white) civilization and (brown) barbarism" remain intact. The boundaries between rich and poor remain intact. The love of war and exaltation of the solider and idolization of the nation . . . they all remain intact, because violence remains the go-to solution, which, in the real world, always seems to translate into "might makes right." For Christians, I would remind us, our sovereign was nailed to an imperial executioner's cross without a fight.

The faux-feminism, the consumer-feminism, the neoliberal-feminism that is valorized by the media—who are part of the power structure—is all about "personal choice." You can be as mean as a male, as rich as a male, as violent as a male, as horny as a male . . . oh, and you can still be sexy. "Femininity" becomes a (sexual) source of "power." Power is recoded to mean what I can do and get and get away with, not what is available to all women, not what is ethical, certainly not political beyond the politics of "personal choice." Self-objectification is back, renamed now as "power." You can have it all, a push-up bra so you can self-objectify—because that's fun, and fun is what matters—and a gun, so you can kick ass just like the boys, who will still find you fuckable. If you can't, it's your own fault, because you just didn't measure up in the undisturbed competitive rat race of sexualized-gender and consumer capitalism.

> One of the problematic assumptions of postfeminist discourse is that women can 'have it all' if only they put their minds to it or try hard enough, which reframes women's struggles and accomplishments as a purely personal matter, thus obscuring the social and material constraints faced by different groups of women. Ironically, this represents a backsliding on . . . feminists' efforts to put the 'personal as political' on the social agenda. Concomitantly, there seems to be an inward-looking focus, and contentment only in the achievement of personal freedoms and fulfilment. A self-focused 'me-feminism' of this sort shifts attention away from the collective 'we-feminism' needed for a transformational political program.[14]

Similarly, there is a problem with so-called "sex-positive" feminism, which has become a code-word for pro-pornography "feminism" (an oxymoron if I ever heard one) in opposition to feminists who *accurately* see the vast majority of pornography as an organized and lucrative male-dominated *industry* that relentlessly cranks out a *woman-hating ideology* that is merged with the brains of ever younger men and boys (and increasingly more young

14. Lazar, "Feminist Critical Discourse Analysis," 154.

women), from an early age, which will come back on the women those men and boys know, and which by the way emotionally and ethically cripples boys and men as the allies, partners, and friends of women.

The term "sex-positive" obfuscates all the ways that sex, as a practice, is inevitably inflected by (gender as) power in a male-hegemonic society. "Sex-positive" is deployed to highlight its straw-woman opposite as . . . "*sex-negative!*" feminists who dare to question the value of uncritical orgasms. Those bad sex-negative feminists are telling us that sex is bad. This false dichotomy is malicious nonsense, and nonsense that always reflects unexamined privilege. As Michelle Lazar, who has studied this phenomenon in advertising, put it:

> Popular postfeminism . . . is a media-friendly, consumer-oriented discourse, which . . . recuperate[s] socially progressive notions of women's empowerment, agency, and self-determination, and in so doing deflect[s] long-standing . . . feminist criticisms of the advertising industry for its oppression of women in setting up narrow and impossible standards of beauty and social acceptability, and for its perpetuation of exploitative, stereotypical images of women. Postfeminist [cultural production] suggests that patriarchal ideologies of gender in terms of women's powerlessness and oppression are outdated. Instead, this is fast becoming a women's world, in which relations of power are shifting in favour of women. Such representations, however, far from supporting the feminist cause, are quite detrimental to it. Feminists' concern for women's empowerment is appropriated and recontextualized by [media], evacuating it of its political content and instead infusing meanings quite antithetical to feminism . . . Structurally, the gender order remains dualistic and hierarchical, but the players have been switched. There appears to be at work a perverse sense of equality—if women traditionally have been the subordinated group, and in the media sexually objectified, it is a sign of social progress to turn the tables on men along similar lines. This is hardly the kind of gender order restructuring envisaged by feminists of any persuasion.[15]

This trend toward "power femininity" loses the term "feminism" and replaces it with—what a surprise—"femininity" . . . again. Gender, that power structure with all its sexual stereotypes, carried on the

15. Ibid., 159.

masculinity-femininity dipole, is restored through its intensified sexualization. Along with "power," a sort of mental-energy Pepsi-generation-ish abracadabra.

The reason feminists said, "The personal is the political," is because they recognized—first hand often enough—the ways in which the public-private dichotomy, in our thinking and in law, worked against women. In its origins, the "public" sphere was exclusively and self-consciously male, as was the arena in which men negotiated power among themselves—the political sphere. The private sphere, the home, was not subject to the public sphere's power in the same ways.[16]

"A man's home is his castle," as they said. And in the home, all those ideas about liberty, equality, and fraternity did not apply. The man was the unquestioned ruler of his wife and children. And this included men's unlimited right to sexual access to wives. This notion of "privacy" has subsequently been deployed to protect persons from undue (and often unjust) government incursions into the personal lives of people; but it is not—as feminists pointed out—an unqualified good. The private sector is anything to which the (public) law is blind. That is why this *sphere*, not "privacy," is an issue of deep concern.

While we may have precluded the government from "invading our privacy," the more abstracted notion that what people do in private should be immune from critique—apart from any question of *law*—has been retained in ways that re-individualize sex, and pretend that sex as a practice is not inflected by the collective/social power of men over women. Rosalind Gill explains what she calls the "sexualization of culture" and the ways women are (again!) encouraged to internalize pornography-fueled, heterosexual male norms.

> The humorous tone that characterised early examples of this shift—e.g. the amusing bra adverts in which billboard models confidently and playfully highlighted their sexual power or traffic-stopping sexiness—should not imply that this shift is not, in fact, profoundly serious and problematic. In the last decade it has gone from being a new and deliberate representational strategy used *on women* (i.e. for depicting young women) to being widely and popularly taken up *by women* as a way of constructing the self: TV presenter Denise van Outen 'confides' in a TV interview, "I do have

16. I'm also keenly aware of Patricia Hill Collins's critique of the white feminist experience of the public-private dichotomy, which I am including prominently in a (hopefully) future book on the public-private dichotomy.

> a lovely pair. I hope they'll still be photographing my tits when I'm 60"; 'readers wives' write in to lad magazines with their favourite sexual experiences e.g. "he turned me around, bent me over the railings and took me from behind, hard"; and girls and women in the west queue up to buy T-shirts with slogans such as 'porn star', 'fcuk me,' and 'fit chick unbelievable knockers'.
>
> To be critical of the shift is not to be somehow 'anti-sex'—though in postfeminist media culture this position (the prude) is the only alternative discursively allowed (itself part of the problem, and eradicating a space for critique). Rather it is to point to the dangers of such representations of women in a culture in which sexual violence is endemic, and to highlight the exclusions of this representational practice—only *some* women are constructed as active, desiring sexual subjects: women who desire sex with men (except when lesbian women 'perform' for men) and only young, slim and beautiful women. As Myra Macdonald (1995) has pointed out, older women, bigger women, women with wrinkles, etc. are never accorded sexual subjecthood and are still subject to offensive and sometimes vicious representations. Indeed, the figure of the unattractive woman who wants a sexual partner remains one of the most vilified in a range of popular cultural forms. Above all, to critique this is to highlight the pernicious connection of this representational shift to neoliberal subjectivities in which sexual objectification can be (re-) presented not as something done to women by some men, but as the freely chosen wish of active, confident, assertive female subjects . . .
>
> Notions of choice, of 'being oneself', and 'pleasing oneself' are central to the postfeminist sensibility that suffuses contemporary Western media culture. They resonate powerfully with the emphasis upon empowerment and taking control that can be seen in talk shows, advertising and makeover shows. A grammar of individualism underpins all these—such that even experiences of racism or homophobia or domestic violence are framed in exclusively personal terms in a way that turns the idea of the personal as political on its head. Lois McNay has called this the deliberate 'reprivatisation' of issues that have only relatively recently become politicised.[17]

While conservative patriarchs and quite radical feminists disagree on the question of whether gender as a power structure is just or unjust, they both agree—contrary to many liberals—that sex, even as a so-called consensual practice, should *not* be immune from critique.

17. Gill, "Postfeminist Media Culture," 8–10.

In unprincipled arguments against sex-critical (not "sex-negative" or "anti-sex") feminists, "postfeminists" have employed guilt-by-association fallacies to misrepresent sex-critical feminists. The fear-mongering on this account is that by approaching the subject of sex critically as a practice, and with an eye to power dynamics, we open the door to censorship and/or policing people's bedrooms.[18] This is an intentional misrepresentation of the methods and motives of sex-critical feminists, and it is a guilt-by-association fallacy. This fallacy has outcomes, one of which is that sex, which feminism was beginning to demystify through power analyses, is being re-mystified as a kind of highly-individualized, magical (or "natural") flux of desire, again dividing nature and culture, and letting culture—which *does* give shape to sexual desire, including eroticizing hatred, aggression, and even violence—off the hook. Feminists put sex into the public (political) sphere, only to have postfeminists try and take it back out again.[19] Post-feminism is liberal feminism boiled down into an absurdity.

This is how we end up saying nonsensical things like, "Rape is not about sex, it is about power." Of course, it is about sex, but if we are to immunize sex from any association *with* or analysis *of* power, then we have to valorize some non-existent, abstracted version of "sex" that exists in a parallel universe where it is *not* inflected by power, in order to continue to point out that rape, as coercive, violent sex, is wrong. So sex cannot be thus immunized. More than ever, we need to be "sex-critical," as opposed to "sex-positive" or "sex-negative."

Most Christians are already sex-critical, but it is a Janus-faced criticism: on the one hand, sex is criticized from a reactionary standpoint in an attempt to reestablish any lost authority to men; and on the other hand, sex is rightly criticized when instrumental as bad faith between persons, using another for selfish ends, which is the opposite of *agape*.[20] We are overdue to

18. This is, in a real sense, a default to bourgeois "democratic" norms and logic, based on the idea that all social change is effected and effective solely through the legislative process, which requires subordinating inconvenient truths and criticisms to the tactics of advancing or protecting a narrow legal goal—passing laws or preventing the passage of laws. This is the strategic mindset, one that I critiqued as male in *Borderline*, and which inevitably subordinates truth-telling to manipulative efficacy.

19. The greatest benefactors of this cooptation have been . . . men. All change can be mitigated, in the minds of many men, if the end result is greater access to women's bodies. Gaining women's active participation is actually a big plus from this standpoint.

20. The latter a criticism with which, as a Christian, I happen to agree; but for which—as a nonviolent Christian—I would not attempt to enforce by law/violence.

set aside the former and pick up the latter, putting Christians and feminists (not necessarily exclusive) into conversation with one another.

Let's do a sex-critical thought experiment. A woman is judged by her looks, objectified and/or dismissed, routinely cajoled and coerced in ways that fall short of the legal definition of rape, and is often put in the position of such dependency on men, or a man, that she feels compelled to give some man sexual access to her body whether she likes it or not. How is power exercised here?

When we become sex-critical, and factor in power analyses, we have to come out of that "sex-positive" denial into the real world where sex is an integral part of relationships that are characterized by control, abuse, pathological possessiveness, and chronic entrapment for women; and the world in which, even in the best of heterosexual relationships (which are mapped onto same-sex relations with gendered dipoles like butch-femme or tops and bottoms), the comparative power of men over women is an issue which, left unacknowledged and un-negotiated, infiltrates those relationships with traumatic consequences.

Real women, by and large, are *not* faced with the option to become powerful honorary males. Nonetheless, they continue to be casualties of the very power structures and practices that are historically male, even when some women who become honorary males are at the helm of institutions. Those institutions operate through agonal competition, authoritarian control, and the threat or use of violence—all associated with a foundational form of "masculinity" which, when opened up to a few women, remains un-critiqued, unchanged, and lacking in all moral intelligence.

Wendy Lynne Lee, of Bloomberg University puts it like this:

> The liberal feminist project cannot fail to risk the self-defeat that accrues to retaining a conceptual framework—the master's tools—that systematically inferiorizes [most actual] women, and diminishes [most actual] women's work. The merely cosmetic improvement produced in some women's lives . . . fails to address the very real life and death issues—the having and rearing of children, for example, which confront women locally, nationally, and globally. Equipped with this insight . . . feminists undertook the conceptual, social, and political quest to comprehend how the subordination of women has become institutionalized, and how this varies with respect to class, ethnicity, culture, ability, age, sexual orientation, and institutions. Late feminist philosopher

> Audre Lorde put it, "The master's tools cannot be used to dismantle the master's house."[21]

This has special implications for Christians who profess nonviolence, given that the films that we reviewed were all films in which women were "elevated" in social standing specifically *by* violence. Not only does this trope of honorary male woman who redeems through violence (Karen Crowder excepted) hardly relate to the reality of most women's lives, and not only does this trope efface the fact that women are disproportionately the *victims* of violence (the exception in the United States being gun homicides), it sets up fictional narratives precisely to justify the use of violence in ways that become a kind of epistemological reality for the most impressionable—young people. Continuing with Lee:

> [T]he notion "equality" is itself tethered to a view of human nature which so privileges attributes traditionally associated with men, such as aggression, hierarchical forms of organization, rugged individualism, competition, and ethical systems that strongly favor impersonal rule-following over relationality, that women are only able to be included within such conceptual frameworks as honorary men . . . examples offered to young women as role models and heroines are modeled after male heroes. The accomplishments of . . . movie heroines like those found in *Terminator II, Aliens, Femme Nikita, The Hunger Games,* or *The Girl with the Dragon Tattoo* . . . are valued according to a standard that rewards domination over domesticity, conquest over caring, and militarism over mothering, in short, masculinity over femininity . . . to reinforce a male-centered or masculinist vision of the good [rather than] a vision centered around values identified as feminine such as cooperation, compromise, collective decision-making, or compassion . . . such programs . . . succeed . . . only at the cost of continuing to devalue qualities associated with femininity, and hence with women.[22]

I hasten to add, "feminine" qualities associated with following the Christ.

Lee is not calling for the "reactive valorization of femininity," as Jessica Benjamin called it earlier in the book, which remains problematic in the way that it separates men and women in gender's power structures, but that this reiteration of the (traditionally male) notion of redemptive violence simultaneously re-inscribes the masculine-feminine dipole, and therefore

21. Lee, ""Feminist Theory: Radical Lesbian," para. 4–5.

22. Ibid., para. 6.

the (traditionally male) power structure, and continues then to devalue most *actual* women.

This raises the question: should the aim of any social transformation of the relationship between men and women be aimed at a kind of heat-death diffusion of all characteristics and values between biological men and women (the erasure of difference), or is the transformation we seek dependent on eliminating to the extent possible the characteristics associated with "masculine" domination and violence?

What has been wrong with patriarchy and its associated social practices has not been that what was done was done *by men*, but that very much of what men did, in exercising unearned power, was *wrong*. We have a lot to answer for. Power empowers the powerful to get away with doing things that are wrong. It's the magic ring we can't control.

Perhaps "equality," for some, in the exercise of power, is not where we ought to be aiming. Patriarchy or andrarchy, whichever we choose to call it, did not evolve as otherwise just forms of power with the sole problem being men's rule over women.

For Christians, in particular, any form of power that strips another of the essential status of a child of God, any form of power that objectifies and/or exploits another child of God, should be an "issue." That is why feminism, as an emancipatory project, is perfectly consistent with Christian witness, whereas a liberally curtailed "feminism," as a project that promotes greater participation in evil by some women, ought to be fairly problematic. If men beating up, torturing, and killing other people is wrong; it is still wrong when women do it.

Walter Brueggemann writes:

> Jesus in his solidarity with the marginal ones is moved to compassion. Compassion constitutes a radical form of criticism, for it announces that the hurt is to be taken seriously, that the hurt is not to be accepted as normal and natural but is an abnormal and unacceptable condition for humanness. In the arrangement of "lawfulness" in Jesus' time, as in the ancient empire of Pharaoh, the one unpermitted quality of relation was compassion. Empires are never built or maintained on the basis of compassion. The norms of law (social control) are never accommodated to persons, but persons are accommodated to norms. Otherwise the norms will collapse and with them the whole power arrangement. Thus the compassion of Jesus is to be understood not simply as a personal emotional reaction but as a public criticism in

> which he dares to act upon his concern against the entire numbness of his social context.[23]

If you ever want to mobilize contempt, just express compassion for a despised category or group, and watch the opposite of vulnerability—hard-heartedness—come to the fore. The I-can-be-meaner-than-he-can game is a man's game, a game of probative masculinity. It's a power game, a game of breaking the mirror of that person who reflects your treatment of them back to you.

Alasdair MacIntyre, in reflecting on men's fear of (our natural, human) vulnerability, a fear expressed in multiple ways from Aristotle to Nietzsche to Donald Trump, wrote, "Such men [men who acknowledge their own dependency and vulnerability] behave as women do." And we know how bad that is. "Those who are manly prefer not to inflict their [vulnerability] by sharing it with [others]. Yet what we should by now have learned from the *virtues of acknowledged dependence* is that this is a respect in which men need to become more like women."[24]

There is no hidden claim here that men are *naturally* aggressive and hard-hearted or that women are *naturally* passive and sentimental. In fact, MacIntyre is clear that what we become is substantially determined by influences we are subjected to from culture and its specificities in location, history, stories, practices, and relations. He says that (most) men need to become more like (most) women with regard to these polarities of hostility and empathy, suggesting that he believes it is possible and not circumscribed by some mechanical version of biology. Not because women are "better" than men, though circumstantially women's roles make them more moral overall than men,[25] but because much of what men think and do from the standpoint of normative males is stupid, destructive, and unhealthy for themselves, their neighbors, and their communities.

Gender did not divide the Good Stuff from the Bad Stuff and give the Good Stuff to men and the Bad Stuff to women. Gender has always operated as a structure that hands men power over women in order to exploit women. The project—spoken or unspoken, understood or mystified—of establishing the exploitative power of one class over another (in this case, men over

23. Brueggemann, *Prophetic Imagination*, 88.

24. MacIntyre, *Dependent Rational Animals*, 164; italics added.

25. Men have, in fact, shirked some of the most crucial social responsibilities related to the care of others, in order to pursue pleasure and power; then devalued that responsibility ("women's work") as justification.

women) does not require a division of moral goods, but the adoption of the tactics and techniques of domination—which are inherently morally questionable. Male monopolization of the kinds of practices required to hold and maintain power (a moral negative) allows men to expropriate various material goods—from sex to money to free labor to rental wombs—for their own aggrandizement or pleasure. This is the very definition of moral turpitude in persons and injustice in social relations. The women are doing the most good, with the most work, and the men are in myriad ways creating the worst problems and skimming the bennies.

Feminism's main breakthroughs have begun with showing concretely what men do to women, as opposed to relying on the kinds of abstractions that underwrite gender as power—gauzy notions of masculine and feminine undisturbed by any whiff of rigorous thought. Gender is never gender alone, because it is nested, or genetically fused with capitalism, a male phenomenon throughout its instigation and development, and a phenomenon that still requires the vicious "virtues" shared by men's war and men's accounting. Masculinized practices demand a self-serving and often cruel instrumentalism from its practitioners, selfishness and instrumentalism now seen too often as masculine "virtues."

And here is where I must address Christians most directly, especially men. Christian theologians and philosophers have been quick to mobilize everything from Plato to Derrida to show how problematic modernity is. I generally agree with this critique; but when it comes to sex-gender, we have a problem.

Feminists themselves have described the ways in which modernity *itself* has taken women out of a frying pan and tossed them into the fire. So far so good. Then we have Wendell Berry or Ivan Illich,[26] whose criticisms of modernity have been stunningly on point in areas *apart from sex-gender*. They acknowledge the ways in which modernity has been bad for women (like rape culture, the pornographication of culture, etc.), then revert to fundamentally reactionary calls for a return to the sex-gender structures of the past . . . claiming that it is "safer" in the frying pan than the fire. I can't read minds, so I am not sure yet whether this reaction is based on the unconscious depth of gender indoctrination that precludes us from imagining any third way; or male Christian intellectuals' personal attachment to their own imagination of an ideal heteronormative complementarity; or the fact

26. Both Christian men.

that their imaginations are limited from reading almost exclusively other male luminaries. Probably all of the above.

In any case, while this may make for uncomfortable alliances, for example, between feminists and Christians who are critical of pornography, it leaves the larger questions underwriting each position unresolved. In my own conversations with other Christian men, what stands out in most cases is that, in addition to clinging to the complementarity of past doctrine, and despite the fact than many Christian men in the academy or pastorate are extremely well read, e.g., in (male) philosophy, there has been next to no commitment to a real and extensive reading and understanding by these same men of feminist thought.[27] In some part, this might be a tendency to believe that feminism is what it is portrayed as by media, and so these men are often content to read *about* feminist thinkers without actually studying those thinkers for themselves.

Yes, the pornographication of culture, etc., is a bad thing (the fire outside the frying pan), but the solution is not to return to the sexual protection racket of the past—one man chosen as protection from all men—even if that hypothetical man is a "benevolent" ruler.

It is true that sex is never "only" sex, and that promiscuity, for example, is harmful for a long list of reasons apart from rules; but the issue is not "feminine virtue" (which implicitly regards women as property).

The issue remains that sex is still invariably wrapped up with power, that intimacy and the casual use of other persons for personal gratification are antithetical, and that what "turns us on" is conditioned by a culture that hates, objectifies, fetishizes, and exploits women. The issue is how often so many men associate sex with fantasies of women's humiliation, domination, hostility, depersonalizing fetishism, and revenge.

This, and not our more voyeuristic preoccupations, is what deserves our attention. Resistance to patriarchy—as perverse power—is our duty every bit as much as resistance to racism, greed, and war.

With that, let me close, with gratitude for your engagement.

27. And nowadays, that means what contact there is with feminism is of the most constructivist postmodern varieties, as postmodernism has become a kind of academic dogma, wherein "second wave" is an epithet indicating one is insufficiently "with it," or out of fashion.

I want to emphasize in the end that I am not saying women should not aspire to do things mostly men do. *It's not my place to tell women anything.* Key influential roles exist in every complex society; but those roles' importance makes them differently valuable to those who cherish their own power. There is nothing wrong with women doing things that men do, including these influential things. More than half my doctors have been women; and that is a good thing altogether.

Those roles cannot be fulfilled for any common good as long as classes of people (like men) retain control not out of a deep vocational desire to see their own communities flourish, but to retain the privileges of power, whereupon the role itself—not the mission—becomes perverse. And nothing could be more perverse than the idea that violence might be our highest civic virtue.

No vice is more dangerous than disregard for human life.

> *Our Savior is our true Mother in whom we are endlessly born and out of whom we shall never come.*
>
> —Julian of Norwich

Bibliography

Banks, Taunya Lovell. "Michael Clayton: Women Lawyers Betrayed—Again." In *Feminism at the Movies: Understanding Gender in Contemporary Popular Cinema*, edited Hilary Radner and Rebecca Stringer, 110–20. New York: Routledge, 2011.

Barber, Nicholas. "The film Star Wars stole from." *BBC*, January 4, 2016. http://www.bbc.com/culture/story/20160104-the-film-star-wars-stole-from.

Bell, Caryn Cossé. "Haitian Immigration to Louisiana in the Eighteenth and Nineteenth Centuries." University of Massachusetts—Lowell, 2000. http://www.inmotionaame.org/texts/viewer.cfm?id=5_000T&page=1.

Bell-Metereau, Rebecca. "Woman: The Other Alien in Alien." In *Women Worldwalkers: New Dimensions of Science Fiction and Fantasy*, edited by Jane B. Weedman, 9–24. Lubbock: Texas Tech Press, 1985.

Bender, Jacob. "Lessons from the Three Wise Men." *The Wisdom Fund*, December 20, 2003. http://www.twf.org/News/Y2003/1220-WiseMen.html.

Benjamin, Jessica. *Bonds of Love: Psychoanalysis, Feminism, and the Problem of Domination*. New York: Pantheon, 1988.

Biography.com. "Author—Susan Collins." September 21, 2016. https://www.biography.com/people/suzanne-collins-20903551.

Bonner, Mehera. "10 Reasons Katniss Should Have Chosen Gale Over Peeta In the Hunger Games." *Teen Vogue*, November 13, 2015.

Brueggemann, Walter. *The Prophetic Imagination*. Minneapolis: Fortress, 2001.

Capetown Trust Rape Crisis. "Rape Trauma Syndrome." http://rapecrisis.org.za/rape-trauma-syndrome/.

Carroll, Lauren. "10 times Hillary Clinton was asked about running for president." Politifact, May 5, 2016. http://www.politifact.com/truth-o-meter/article/2016/may/05/10-times-hillary-clinton-was-asked-about-running-p/.

Châteauvert-Gagnon, Béatrice. "From Militarized Femininity to Female Masculinity: Women Soldiers in American War Movies." Conference Presentation. *Université du Québec à Montréal*, March 29, 2013. http://sussex.academia.edu/BeatriceChateauvertGagnon.

Clover, Carol. *Men, Women, and Chain Saws: Gender in the Modern Horror Film*. Princeton: Princeton University Press, 1992.

———. "Her Body, Himself: Gender in the Slasher Film." *Representations* (Autumn 1987) 187–228.

Creed, Barbara. “Horror and the Monstrous Feminine.” *Screen* (January/February 1986) 67–76.

———. *The Monstrous Feminine: Film, Feminism, Psychoanalysis.* New York: Routledge, 1993.

Department of State. “Lithuania: 2016 Trafficking in Persons Report.” https://www.state.gov/j/tip/rls/tiprpt/countries/2016/258808.htm.

Dietel, David. “*Alien*: a Film Franchise Based Entirely on Rape.” *Cracked.com*, January 2, 2011. http://archive.li/ppCJF.

Dinello, Dan. “The Contagious Age: Overwhelmed by Vampires, Viruses, and Zombies in the 21st Century.” *Pop Matters*, September 7, 2001. https://www.popmatters.com/148166-the-contagious-age-overwhelmed-by-vampires-viruses-and-zombies-2495957745.html?rebelltitem=1#rebelltitem1.

Dominus, Susan. “Susan Collins's War Stories for Kids.” *New York Times Magazine*, April 8, 2011. https://www.nytimes.com/2011/04/10/magazine/mag-10collins-t.html.

Dublin, Thomas. “Women and the Industrial Revolution in the United States.” *The Gilder Lehrman Institute of American History.* https://ap.gilderlehrman.org/essay/women-and-early-industrial-revolution-united-states.

Dworkin, Andrea. Our Blood—Prophecies and Discourses on Sexual Politics, 12. New York: Perigree, 1976.

Eckert, Penelope. “The whole woman: Sex and gender differences in variation.” *Language Variation and Change* 1 (1989) 253–54.

Ellis, Phillip. “Before Her Lambs Were Silent.” In *Dissecting Hannibal Lecter*, edited by Benjamin Szumskyj, 160–75. Jefferson, NC: McFarland, 2008.

Evans, Megan. “Silence of the Sexes.” *Undergraduate Research Journal.* University of Central Florida, January 11, 2010. https://www.urj.ucf.edu/docs/evans.pdf.

Fabello, Melissa. “Breaking down the assumption that some women go for jerks.” *Everyday Feminism*, December 31, 2012. https://everydayfeminism.com/2012/12/but-why-do-some-women-go-for-aholes/.

Farmer, Paul. *The Uses of Haiti.* Monroe, ME: Common Courage, 2003.

Gallardo, Ximena, and Jason Smith. *Alien Woman: the Making of Lieutenant Ellen Ripley.* London: Bloomsbury, 2004.

Gill, Rosalind. “Postfeminist media culture: elements of a sensibility.” *European Journal of Cultural Studies* 10 (2007) 147–66.

Goff, Stan. *Borderline: Reflections on War, Sex, and Church.* Eugene, OR: Cascade, 2015.

Goldman, Robert. *Reading Ads Socially.* New York: Routledge. 1992.

Haggstrom, Jason. “Reassessing *Alien.*” *Reel* 3, June 8, 2012. http://reel3.com/reassessing-alien-sexuality-and-the-anxieties-of-men/.

Herman, Alison. “Mothers of the Rebellion.” *The Ringer*, December 19, 2016. https://www.theringer.com/2016/12/19/16040550/the-women-of-star-wars-bbe9fbc8603d.

Holmes, Linda. “What Really Makes Katniss Stand Out? Peeta, Her Movie Girlfriend.” Pop Culture Happy Hour, *NPR*, November 25, 2013, http://www.npr.org/sections/monkeysee/2013/11/25/247146164/what-really-makes-katniss-stand-out-peeta-her-movie-girlfriend.

Huffington Post. “Cameron Diaz: ‘Every woman wants to be objectified.” November 20, 2012. https://www.huffingtonpost.com/2012/11/20/cameron-diaz-every-woman-wants-to-be-objectified_n_2164965.html.

James, C. L. R. *The Black Jacobins: Toussaint L'Overture and the San Domingo Revolution.* New York: Vintage, 1989.

Jennings, Theodore W. *Outlaw Justice: The Messianic Politics of Paul*. Palo Alto, CA: Stanford University Press, 2017.

Kamir, Orit. "Michael Clayton: Hollywood's Contemporary Hero-Lawyer: Beyond 'Outsider Within' and 'Insider Without.'" *Academia*, 2007. http://www.academia.edu/4375291/Michael_Clayton_Hollywoods_Contemporary_Hero-Lawyer_Beyond_Outsider_Within_and_Insider_Without.

Kibbey, Ann. "Gender and the American Ideology of War." *Genders* 37 (2003) https://cdn.atria.nl/ezines/IAV_606661/IAV_606661_2010_51/g37_editorial.html.

Lacan, Jacques. *Écrits*. New York: Norton, 2007.

———. "The Ethics of Psychoanalysis." Lacan Seminar. *Société Parisienne de Psychanalyse*, 1969–60.

———. "The Signification of the Phallus." Lecture presented to the *Max Planck Institute*, Munich, 1958.

Lazar, Michelle M. "Feminist Critical Discourse Analysis: Articulating a Feminist Discourse Praxis." *Critical Discourse Studies* 4 (September 2007) 141–64.

Lee, Joseph. "28 Days Later, where's everybody." *CNN*, August 8, 2003. https://money.cnn.com/2003/08/08/news/companies/28_days_later/index.htm.

Lee, Wendy Lynne. "Feminist Theory: Radical Lesbian (A Glorious Past and an Ecological Future)." In *International Encyclopaedia of the Social and Behavioral Sciences*, edited by Neil J. Smelzer & Paul M. Bates. Amsterdam: Pergamon, 2001. https://www.academia.edu/11885746/Feminist_Theory_Radical_Lesbian_A_Glorious_Past_and_an_Ecological_Future_.

Linstrom, Kirsti E. "The Submissive, the Angel, and the Mad Woman in District 12: Feminine Identity in Suzanne Collins' s The Hunger Games." *Stephen F. Austin State University*, December 8, 2014. https://scholarworks.sfasu.edu/cgi/viewcontent.cgi?article=1004&context=english_research_methods.

Lueptow, Kelsey. "Is 'Bitch' an Example of Internalized Sexism?" *Everyday Feminism*, February 25, 2014. https://everydayfeminism.com/2014/02/bitch-internalized-sexism/.

MacIntyre, Alasdair. *After Virtue*. Notre Dame: University of Notre Dame, 1984.

———. *Dependent Rational Animals*. London: Bloomsbury, 2009.

Martin, Karl E. "Failure of a Pseudo-Christian Community." *Journal of Religion and Film*, October 1, 2014. https://digitalcommons.unomaha.edu/cgi/viewcontent.cgi?article=1220&context=jrf.

Moi, Toril. "From Femininity to Finitude." *Journal of Women and Culture in Society* (2004) 841–78.

Moreman, Christopher M., and Cory James Rushton. *Race, Oppression and the Zombie: Essays on Cross-cultural Appropriations of the Caribbean Tradition*. Jefferson, NC: McFarland, 2011.

Mosley, Walter. *Black Betty*. New York: Washington Square, 1994.

Mulvey, Laura. "Visual Pleasure and Narrative Cinema." In *Film Theory and Criticism: Introductory Readings*, edited by Leo Braudy and Marshall Cohen, 833–44. New York: Oxford University Press, 1999.

Nakamura, Kevin and J. Wisniewski. "5 Ridiculous Myths Everyone Believes About the Wild West." *Cracked.com*, April 24, 2013. http://www.cracked.com/article_20372_5-ridiculous-myths-everyone-believes-about-wild-west.html.

Ormhaug, Cristin. "Armed Conflict Deaths Disaggregated by Gender." *International Peace Institute—Oslo*, November 23, 2009.

Ovid. *Metamorphoses*, Book VII. Internet Classics Archive, MIT. http://classics.mit.edu/Ovid/metam.html.

Pateman, Carole. *The Sexual Contract*. Palo Alto, CA: Stanford University Press, 1988.

Pollitt, Katha. "The Smurfette Principle." *The New York Times*, April 7, 1991.

Poloczek, Katarzyna. "From the Kitchen to the Bathroom: Feminist (Post) Theory in Crisis." In *Theory that Matters: What Practice After Theory*, edited by Kacper Bartaczak and Malgorzata Myk, 218–36. Newcastle upon Tyne: Cambridge Scholars, 2013.

Rich, Adrienne Cecile. "Compulsory Heterosexuality and Lesbian Existence (1980)." *Journal of Women's History* 15 (Autumn 2003) 11–48. https://muse.jhu.edu/article/48874.

Ristik, Hugh (pseudonym). "Misunderstanding Patriarchy." *Daran's Blog*, December 31, 2006. https://cddaran.wordpress.com/2006/12/31/misunderstanding-patriarchy/.

Samerski, Silya. "Risk-Anxiety and the Myth of Informed Decision Making." University of Bremen, 2002. https://www.pudel.uni-bremen.de/pdf/SamerskiOslokorr.pdf.

Shigematsu, Shetsu, Kristina Bhagwati, and Eli Paintedcrow. "Women-of-color Veterans on war, militarism, and feminism." In *Feminism and War: Confronting US Imperialism*, edited by Robin Riley, Chandra Talpade Mohanty, and Minnie Bruce Pratt, 93–102. London: Zed, 2008.

Silverstein, Melissa. "Why Isn't This a Bigger Issue?" *Women & Hollywood Blog*, February 20, 2008. http://womenandhollywood.blogspot.com/2008/02/why-isnt-this-bigger-issue.html.

Stets, John E., and Peter J. Burke. "Femininity/Masculinity." In *Encyclopedia of Sociology*, edited by Edward F. Borgatta and Rhonda J. V. Montgomery, 977–78. New York: Macmillan, 2000.

Thaller, Sarah. "A Feminist Bait-and-Switch: The Hunger Games and the Illusion of Empowerment." *Parlour*, September 21, 2016. https://www.ohio.edu/parlour/news-story.cfm?newsItem=04A7BBE4-5056-A874-1D563D477E575CA0.

Urbaniak, Jeffrey C., and Peter R. Kilman. "Physical Attractiveness and the Nice Guy Paradox." *Sex Roles* 9 (November 2003) 413–26.

Wein, Elise. "Getting the Joke of White Feminism." *The Dartmouth*, January 25, 2017. http://www.thedartmouth.com/article/2017/01/getting-the-joke-of-white-feminism.

Wink, Walter. *The Powers that Be: Theology for a New Millennium*. New York: Doubleday, 1999.

Wloszczyna, Susan. "'Clayton' revives the conspiracy genre." *USA Today*, October 14, 2007.

Young, John. "Box Office Report: 'The Hunger Games' posts third best opening weekend ever with $155 mil." *Entertainment Weekly*, March 5, 2012.

Žižek, Slavoj. *Looking Awry*. Cambridge: MIT Press, 1991.

Index

www.ingramcontent.com/pod-product-compliance
Lightning Source LLC
LaVergne TN
LVHW051004080826
845145LV00009B/2451

* 9 7 8 1 5 3 2 6 4 4 0 8 5 *